INSTRUCTOR'S MANUAL

to accompany

HOTEL FRONT OFFICE SIMULATION

A WORKBOOK AND SOFTWARE PACKAGE

SHERYL FRIED KLINE AND WILLIAM SULLIVAN

John Wiley & Sons, Inc.

This book is printed on acid-free paper. ∞

Library of Congress Cataloging-in-Publication Data:

ISBN: 0-471-20777-2

CONTENTS

Introduction   **v**
Steps to Print Screen Shots from INNSTAR   v
Role-Playing   vi

Chapter 1   Getting Started   **1**
Chapter Outline   1
Key Learning Concepts in Chapter 1   1
Additional Activities and Exercise Suggestions   1
Answers to Chapter 1 Exercises   1
Transparency Masters   3

Chapter 2   Reservations   **8**
Chapter Outline   8
Key Learning Concepts in Chapter 2   8
Additional Activities and Exercise Suggestions   8
Answers to Chapter 2 Exercises   9
Transparency Masters   11

Chapter 3   Registration   **38**
Chapter Outline   38
Key Learning Concepts in Chapter 3   38
Additional Activities and Exercise Suggestions   39
Answers to Chapter 3 Exercises   41
Transparency Masters

Chapter 4   Posting and Folio Management   **57**
Chapter Outline   57
Key Learning Concepts in Chapter 4   57
Additional Activities and Exercise Suggestions   57
Answers to Chapter 4 Exercises   59
Transparency Masters

Chapter 5   Guest Services   **85**
Chapter Outline   85
Key Learning Concepts in Chapter 5   85
Additional Activities and Exercise Suggestions   85
Answers to Chapter 5 Exercises   86
Transparency Masters   87

Chapter 6   Night Audit   **108**
Chapter Outline   108
Key Learning Concepts in Chapter 6   108
Additional Activities and Exercise Suggestions   108
Answers to Chapter 6 Exercises   108

INTRODUCTION

This **Instructor's Manual** accompanies *Hotel Front Office Simulation: A Workbook and Software Package*. The Workbook takes students from the reservation process through the guest cycle and ends with the night audit. One day in the life a hotel is covered within the Software and Workbook Exercises. The Instructor's Manual is intended to aid the instructor with guiding students through the Workbook and Software.

Each chapter includes the following: Chapter Outline, Key Learning Concepts, Additional Activities and Exercise Suggestions, Answers to Chapter Exercises, and Transparency Masters. Additionally, the Workbook figures and additional Exercise figures are available in PowerPoint. These presentations can be downloaded from **www.wiley.com/college**. These materials are helpful when using this software in the classroom. In addition to using the Additional Activities and Exercise Suggestions in this manual, we also encourage instructors to explore the different functions of the software and create your own assignments to fit the needs of your course. The INNSTAR software package is a real property management system (PMS) and can be used to demonstrate many aspects of a PMS.

Steps to Print Screen Shots from INNSTAR

In addition to using the exercises in the Workbook, instructors may also want students to hand in print outs of their work. Since this is a real PMS system only a limited number of activities may be printed via the print commands. However, students can use the following steps to print any screen image from the INNSTAR program. A screen image can be captured from any part of the INNSTAR software package. Following is a brief outline of how to print screen shots.

1. To print any screen of INNSTAR the software must be in use. In addition, open a new document in Microsoft Word or any comparable word processing program.

2. Return to the window with INNSTAR and the screen you wish to print. On your keyboard depress the "Print Screen/SysRq" key.

3. Maximize (open) the window for the Microsoft Word document. Or you can toggle between screens by pressing Alt–Tab. Once within Microsoft Word again, select "Paste" from the Edit Menu or depress Control–V. The screen from INNSTAR will appear in the Microsoft Word document. The document can now be printed.

4. If you wish to alter the format of the screen shot, double click on the image. From the format window that opens, you can adjust the size and picture of the image.

This process will permit students to copy any screen from their INNSTAR program. Students may now hand in homework assignments that show exactly what is in their PMS and give the instructor the option of viewing the images from the student's system along with the homework exercises. For example, students can print and hand in copies of reservations, registration information, room racks, and posting statements. This printing process can be used for all chapters and all homework assignments.

Role-Playing

Role-playing is a great way for students to experience the events that occur while using a PMS system and practice the skills needed to understand the guest cycle. Using at least one role-play exercise in the classroom per chapter will promote lively class discussion through this popular experiential teaching technique. It is helpful for the instructor to create a scenario for students to enact. It should give enough detail about a situation so students understand their role but omit information about how to handle a situation.

Following a role-play by students, the instructor should lead a discussion that allows students to react to what happened. Instructors can ask questions and a lead a discussion about what occurred. These questions allow students to process the role-play and explore more fully the situation at hand. Helpful questions to ask include how student's felt during the role-play, what did they do that was effective or ineffective, and what could be done to improve the situation the next time.

The following is an example of using student pairs to role-play a reservation scenario. Students are asked to role-play making a reservation.

Scenario
Students are divided into pairs. For each pair one student plays the reservationist; the other is assigned the part of a guest. The student who plays the reservationist is seated in front of a PC using his or her own INNSTAR software package. The student playing the customer pretends to use a telephone to make a reservation.

A guest calls to make a reservation for his or her family. The family consists of 2 adults and 2 children. The guest would like 2 connecting rooms. The family plans to arrive on November 19 of this year and stay 2 nights.

After the role-play the following are the types of questions that can be asked:

1. What was easy and what was a challenge in playing the reservationist? Think about how the PMS software impacted the reservation process.

2. What did you do that was effective or ineffective?

3. What could be done to improve this interaction next time?

Role-playing may also be performed in front of the class, with other student observing the interaction. It can also be performed using trios of students. Two students perform the role-play and the third student observes the interaction and reports the observations to the class.

Role-playing is a great teaching method and works well with this Workbook.

CHAPTER 1

GETTING STARTED

Chapter Outline

Chapter 1 describes how to use the Workbook and Software. The basics for using the software are covered in detail. The software is easy to use and is keyboard driven. Most students quickly learn to navigate the software from opening the program to logging off. Chapter 1 also has a description of the hotel property, the Sullklin Inn.

Key Learning Concepts in Chapter 1
- Reservations and Room Availability
- Registration
- Guest Room Posting and Check-out
- Guest Services
- Night Audit

Additional Activities and Exercise Suggestions

1. Have students look at the Room Status Scan by pressing the S key from the main menu and then pressing the Page Down key. Discuss the room layout. Note that room 100 is an ADA room. ADA stands for the Americans with Disabilities Act and an ADA room is designed to be handicapped assessable. Also note that rooms 200-208 are smoking rooms and all other rooms are designated non-smoking.

2. Two other screens that may be helpful to students are found in the area of the Front Desk Reports. Press N from the main menu to locate a list of front desk reports. From this screen, press either 1 or 2. Either report will list the guests who are checked in. Discuss with the students that although they have just purchased this hotel and it is new to them, the hotel has been in operation and there are guests occupying some rooms.

3. Go over the concept of rack rate. A rack rate is the highest regular rate the hotel charges guests for a room type.

    The rack rate for the Double Double (DD) bedded rooms is $85, for the King (KING) bedded rooms it is $100 and for the suites (SUIT) it is $200.

Answers to Chapter 1 Exercises

1) a) Sullklin Inn
   b) September 28, 2000

2) Students will provide a variety of answers to this question. They will refer to the property's layout in Figure 1.5 when describing the facility. The history of the property may include when it was built and who owned it. The target markets are business travelers during the week and family clientele on the weekend.

3) Enter key, page up and page down keys, and arrow keys

4) The mouse is not used for any part of this program.

5) The Function or F-keys are located at the top of the keyboard above the number keys.

Transparency Masters for the Chapter 1 Workbook figures can be found beginning the next page.

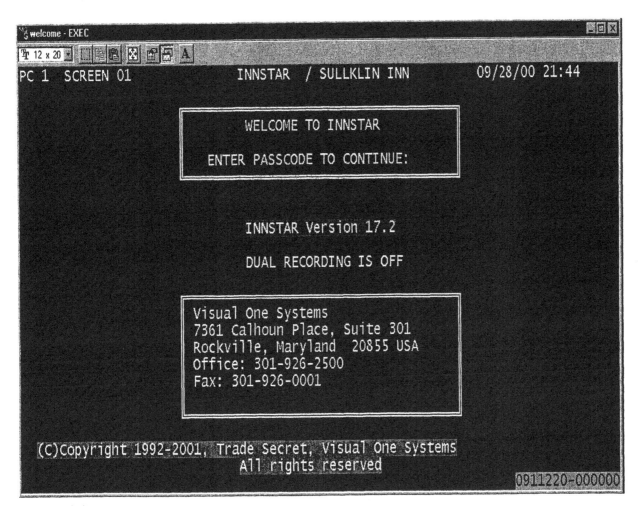

Figure 1.1

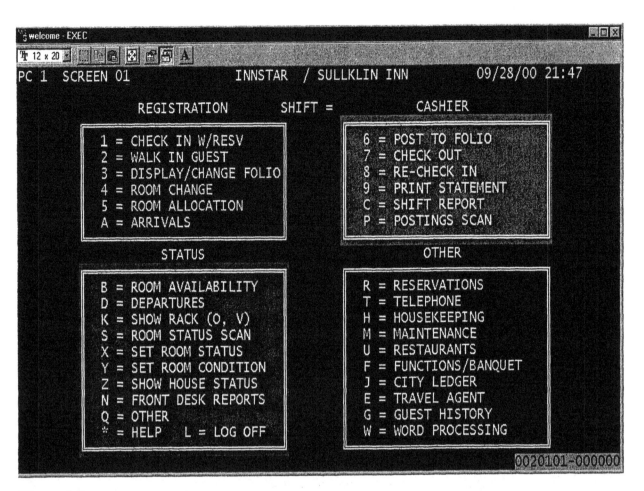

Figure 1.2

4

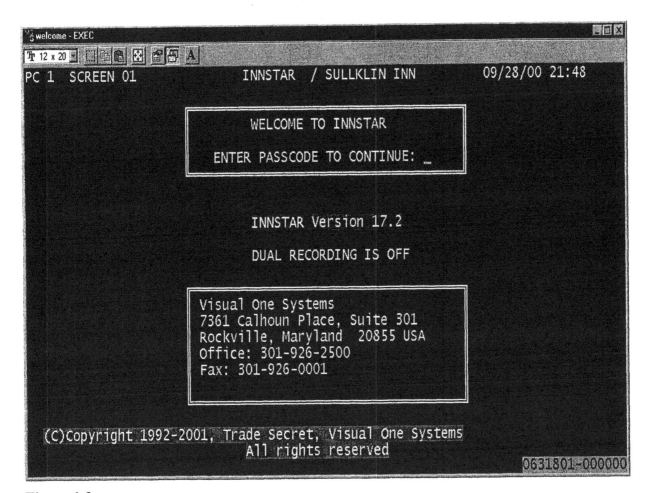

Figure 1.3

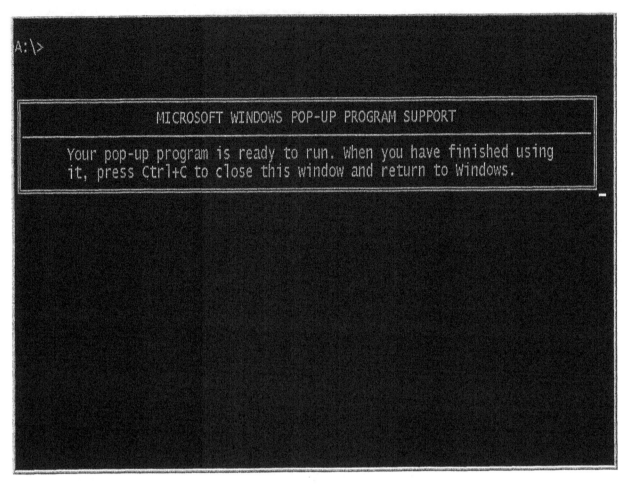

Figure 1.4

Sullklin Inn

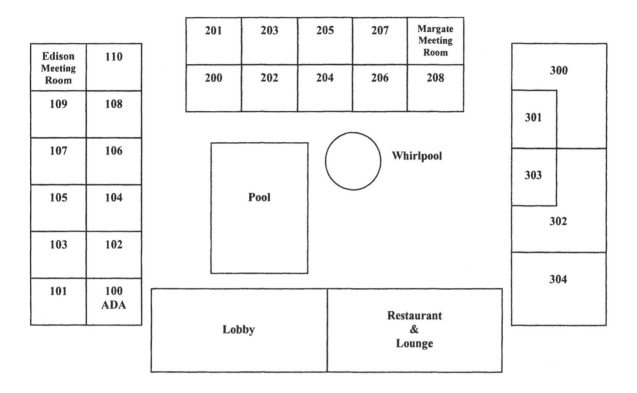

Figure 1.5

CHAPTER 2

RESERVATIONS

Chapter Outline

Chapter 2 describes the reservation process. Students create a variety of reservations and explore special reservation situations. Students use both the individual and group reservation modules. The reservation process includes changing and canceling reservations. Group reservations are created and rooms are picked up from group blocks. Students are exposed to several reservation reports. Room availability, and daily summary screens are analyzed in this chapter.

Key Learning Concepts in Chapter 2
- How to create a reservation
- Steps in the reservation process
- How to retrieve and display a reservation
- How to cancel and reactivate a reservation
- How to make a group block and book a room from a group block
- Describe and analyze the information contained in the room availability, daily summary, and daily booking screens.
- How to handle special reservations issues including share-with and advance deposit functions

Additional Activities and Exercise Suggestions

1) Mr. and Mrs. Handy Kapps would like to make a reservation for February 15 for one night. Mrs. Kapps states that Mr. Kapps is hearing impaired and would like to request a room that is equipped with a TDD telephone and any other special devise that a hearing impaired person would need (special alarm clock, light activated door bell, etc.). Make a reservation for two adults at the rack rate. The Kapps lives at 15 Apple Street, Avenel, NJ 10031. The phone number is 732-555-4553. She would like to use a Master Card to guarantee the room; the number is 5555-9999-8531-3497. Make a reservation for Mr. and Mrs. Kapps. What other special comments or arrangements would you make for this guest?

    Answer: Make the reservation and request room 100 the ADA room. Also place the request for a TDD and other hearing impaired equipment to be placed in the room prior to arrival. Also a student may block this room for the guest.

2) Ms. Suzi Welltraveled is calling from the Welltraveled Travel Agency, 40 Main St Lafayette, IN 47907. The travel agencies phone number is 765-555-5996. She would like to make a reservation for Mr. Mark Manship. Mr. Manship is arriving on February 19 for 2 nights. Ms. Welltraveled will call back with the address and phone information for Mr. Manship when

she has a credit card to guarantee it. How would you handle this reservation?

Answer: Make the reservation and complete the travel agency portion of the reservation leaving the guest information blank. Explain to Ms. Welltraveled that the room is not guaranteed and that a credit card or other payment is required to guarantee the room.

3) Have a student create a group reservation for his or her own family reunion. Choose two nights in the month of February 2001.

Answers to Chapter 2 Exercises

2) In this example the student made a reservation for four nights. Therefore, there are now two suites available on January 1,2,3 and 4. The occupancy percentage is 4% and not zero. The assignment didn't specify how many nights the student reserved the room so their answer may differ based on the number of night's stay.

3) a) The student would go into R for reservation and then press 4 to reactivate the reservation. After pressing 4 the student would type in the letters "Leah" to locate Ms. Leahy's cancelled reservation. Once the student pulls up the reservation they would reconfirm the address to ensure that the correct reservation has been selected. Now change the arrival date to November 29th and complete the reactivation of this reservation.

   b) The student would double check that the correct reservation was selected by asking the guest to reconfirm her address. S/he would also restate the new arrival date and reconfirm the number of nights the guest would like to stay. The student would also reconfirm that that the guest would like to guarantee this reservation with a credit card. S/he would ask the guest to provide the card number again. Finally, the student would thank Mrs. Leahy for her reservation.

4) a) Transient, Standard, and Rack
   b) A sharewith

5) a) The first 4 letters of the guests last name.

6) a) Booking a room is to take a guest's name and information and apply it to a reservation. An example of blocking a room is to hold a number of rooms for a group. Usually the guest's names have not been provided yet but the group is holding a certain number of rooms under the groups name.
      If Mr. Biryani was not part of a group the student would make a reservation using R for Reservation and 1 to enter a reservation for a guest.

   b) The student would enter the information in the comment section.

7) September 30 and October 1
   DD rooms- 10 each night
   King rooms- 10 each night

Suites- 3 each night

    October 5
    DD rooms- minus 1
    King rooms- 1
    Suites- 3

    October 6
    DD rooms- 11
    King rooms- 11
    Suites- 3

8)   5

9)   21

10) 2

11) Question 8—Daily Booking Summary of Rooms Availability
      Question 9—Daily Booking Summary of Rooms Availability
      Question 10—Daily Bookings

Transparency Masters for the Chapter 2 Workbook figures can be found beginning the next page.

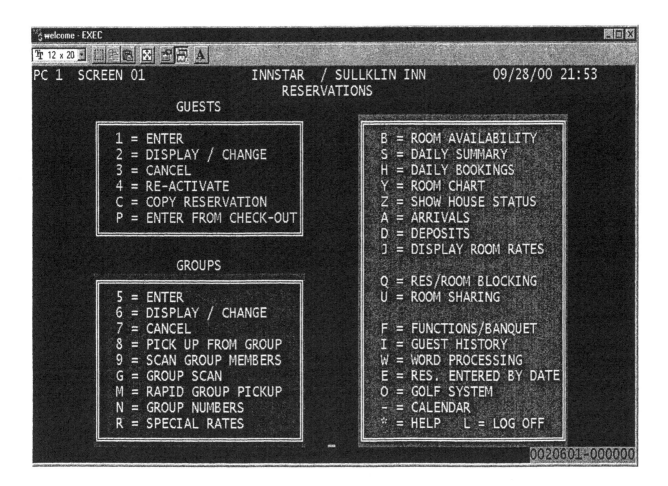

Figure 2.1

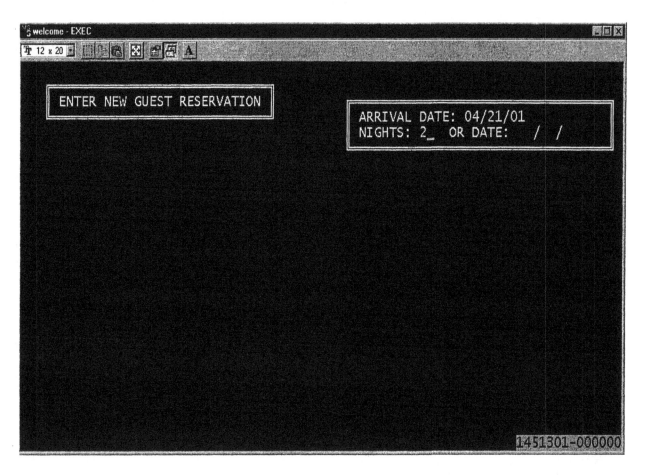

Figure 2.2

12

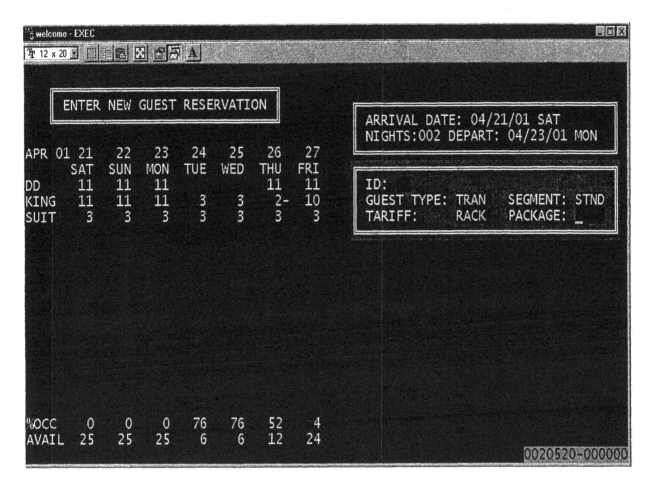

Figure 2.3

13

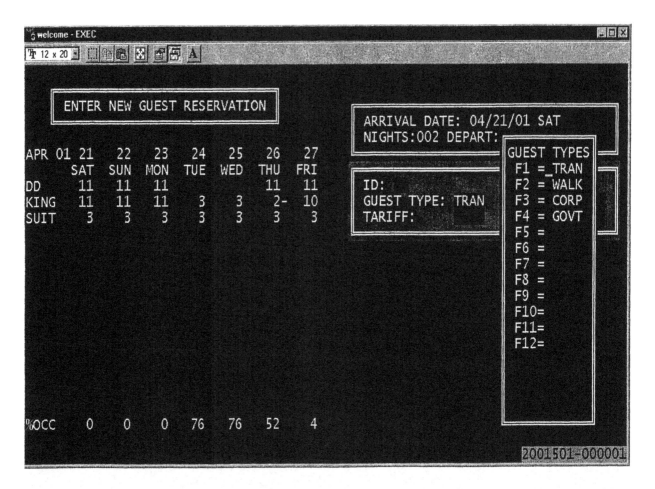

Figure 2.4

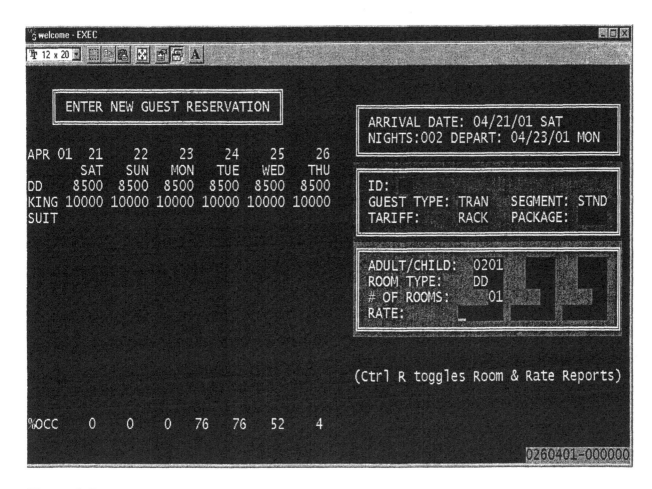

Figure 2.5

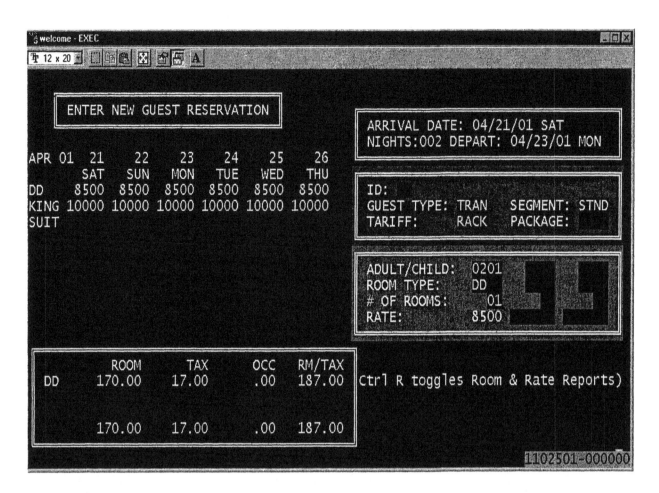

Figure 2.6

16

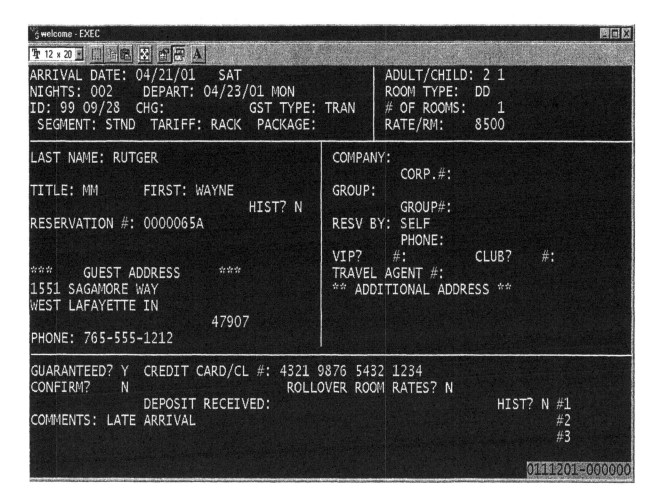

Figure 2.7

17

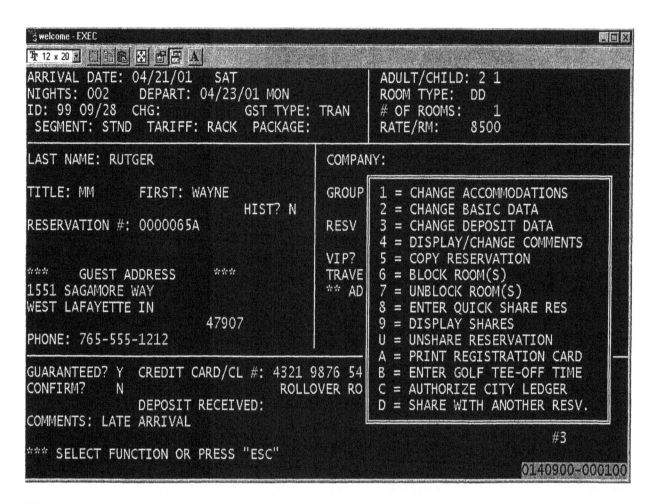

Figure 2.8

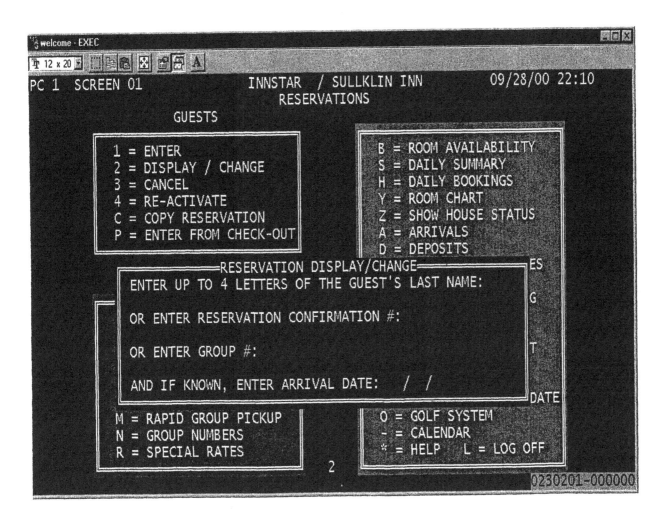

Figure 2.9

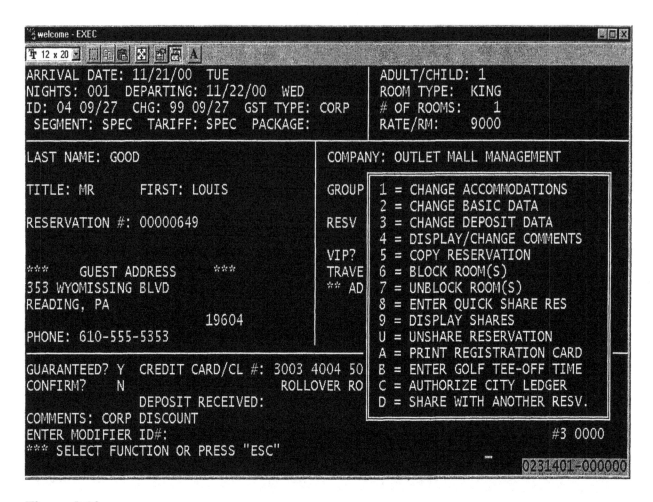

Figure 2.10

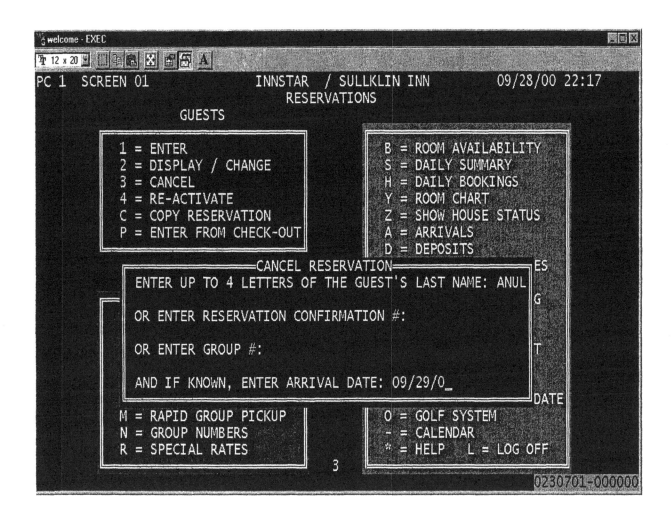

Figure 2.11

21

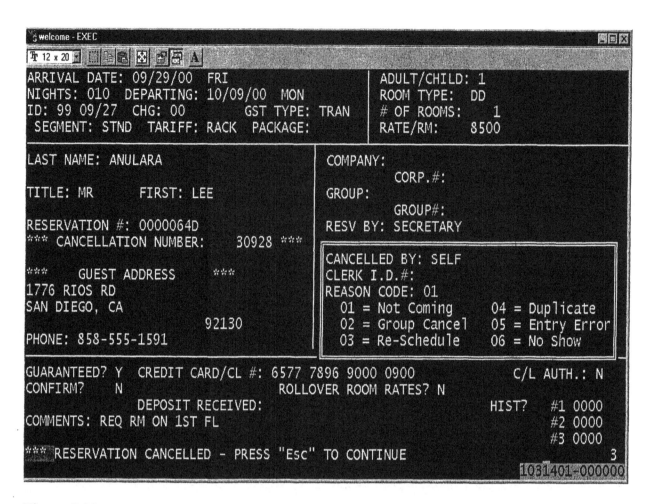

```
 welcome - EXEC                                                    ⬛⬛⬛⬛
 𝕋 12 x 20 ▾  ⬛⬛⬛ ⬛ ⬛⬛ A
ARRIVAL DATE: 09/29/00  FRI            │ ADULT/CHILD: 1
NIGHTS: 010  DEPARTING: 10/09/00  MON  │ ROOM TYPE:  DD
ID: 99 09/27  CHG: 00        GST TYPE: TRAN │ # OF ROOMS:    1
 SEGMENT: STND  TARIFF: RACK  PACKAGE: │ RATE/RM:    8500
───────────────────────────────────────┴─────────────────────
LAST NAME: ANULARA                     COMPANY:
                                               CORP.#:
TITLE: MR      FIRST: LEE              GROUP:
                                               GROUP#:
RESERVATION #: 0000064D                RESV BY: SECRETARY
*** CANCELLATION NUMBER:     30928 ***
                                      ┌────────────────────────────────┐
***    GUEST ADDRESS      ***         │CANCELLED BY: SELF              │
1776 RIOS RD                          │CLERK I.D.#:                    │
SAN DIEGO, CA                         │REASON CODE: 01                 │
                      92130           │  01 = Not Coming   04 = Duplicate│
                                      │  02 = Group Cancel 05 = Entry Error│
PHONE: 858-555-1591                   │  03 = Re-Schedule  06 = No Show  │
                                      └────────────────────────────────┘
GUARANTEED? Y  CREDIT CARD/CL #: 6577 7896 9000 0900        C/L AUTH.: N
CONFIRM?    N                    ROLLOVER ROOM RATES? N
            DEPOSIT RECEIVED:                         HIST?  #1 0000
COMMENTS: REQ RM ON 1ST FL                                   #2 0000
                                                             #3 0000
*** RESERVATION CANCELLED - PRESS "Esc" TO CONTINUE                  3
                                                     1031401-000000
```

Figure 2.12

22

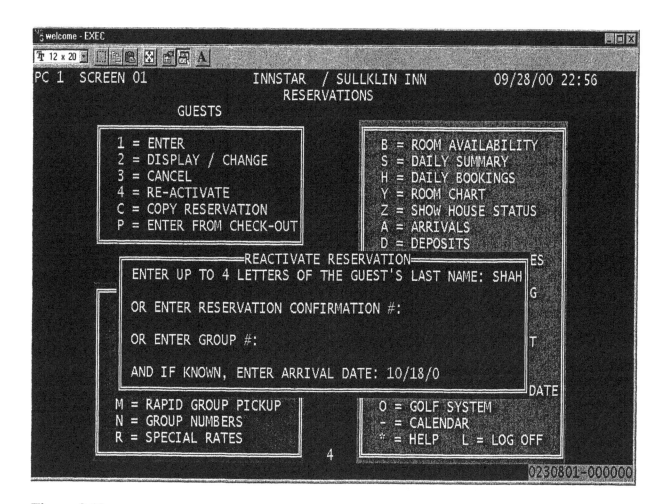

Figure 2.13

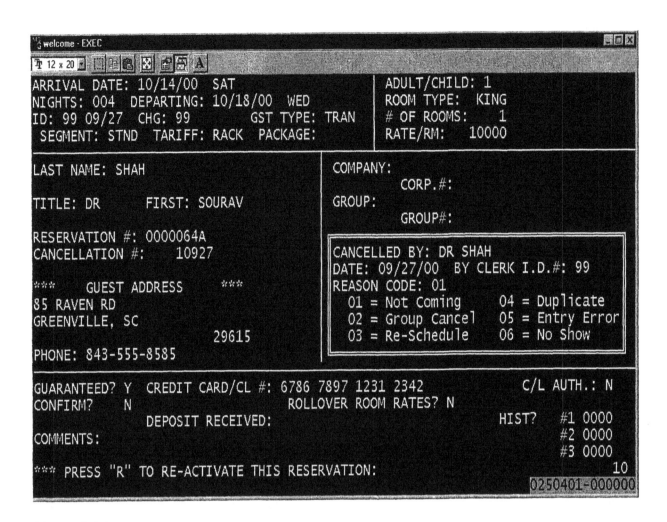

Figure 2.14

24

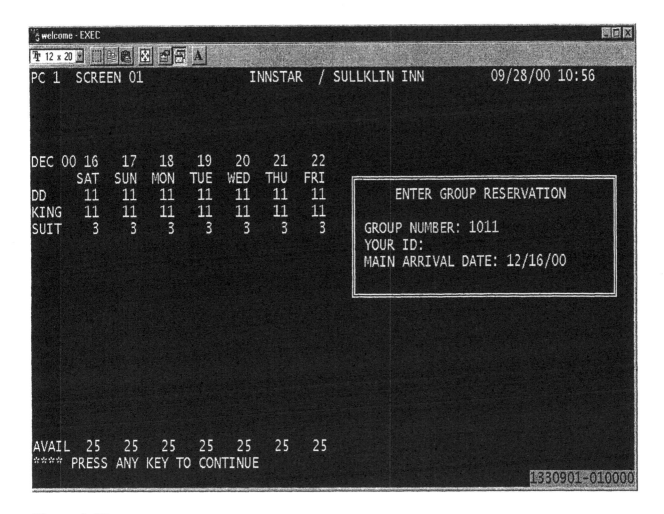

Figure 2.15

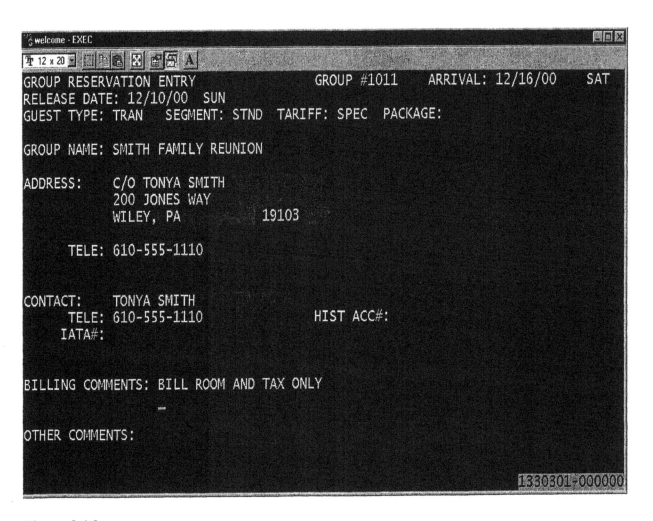

```
welcome - EXEC                                                    _ □ X
Tr 12 x 20    ▦ 🗎🗎 🔳 🗎🗎 A
GROUP RESERVATION ENTRY                  GROUP #1011    ARRIVAL: 12/16/00    SAT
RELEASE DATE: 12/10/00  SUN
GUEST TYPE: TRAN   SEGMENT: STND  TARIFF: SPEC  PACKAGE:


GROUP NAME: SMITH FAMILY REUNION

ADDRESS:    C/O TONYA SMITH
            200 JONES WAY
            WILEY, PA          19103

     TELE: 610-555-1110



CONTACT:    TONYA SMITH
       TELE: 610-555-1110              HIST ACC#:
     IATA#:



BILLING COMMENTS: BILL ROOM AND TAX ONLY


OTHER COMMENTS:

                                                    1330301-000000
```

Figure 2.16

26

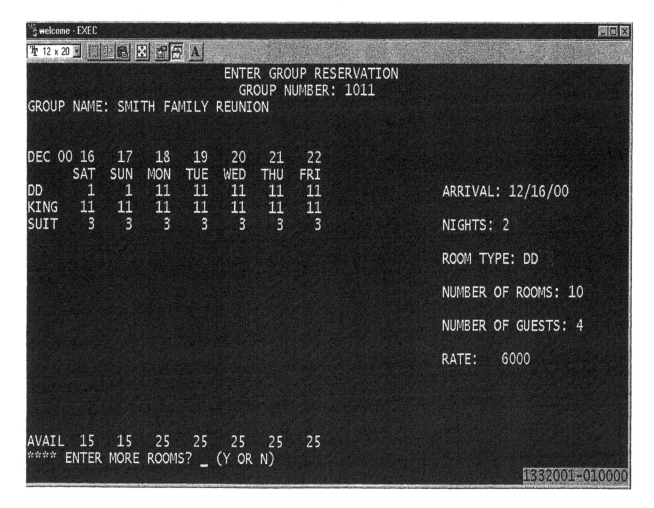

Figure 2.17

27

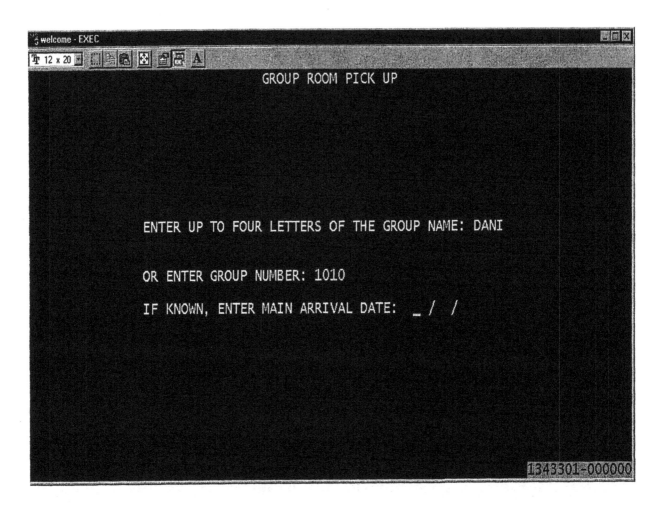

Figure 2.18

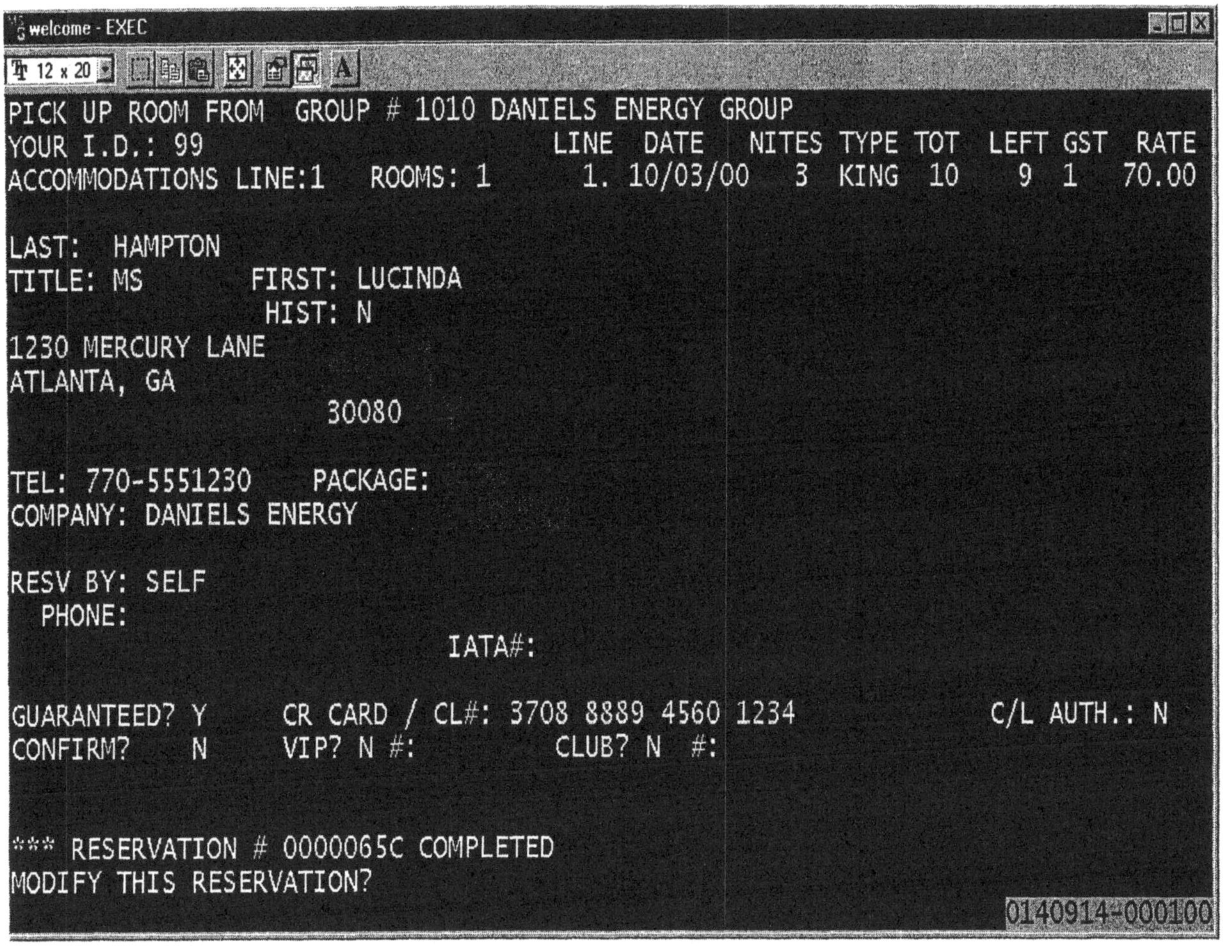
welcome - EXEC
12 x 20
PICK UP ROOM FROM GROUP # 1010 DANIELS ENERGY GROUP
YOUR I.D.: 99 LINE DATE NITES TYPE TOT LEFT GST RATE
ACCOMMODATIONS LINE:1 ROOMS: 1 1. 10/03/00 3 KING 10 9 1 70.00
LAST: HAMPTON
TITLE: MS FIRST: LUCINDA
HIST: N
1230 MERCURY LANE
ATLANTA, GA
30080
TEL: 770-5551230 PACKAGE:
COMPANY: DANIELS ENERGY
RESV BY: SELF
PHONE:
IATA#:
GUARANTEED? Y CR CARD / CL#: 3708 8889 4560 1234 C/L AUTH.: N
CONFIRM? N VIP? N #: CLUB? N #:
*** RESERVATION # 0000065C COMPLETED
MODIFY THIS RESERVATION?
0140914-000100

Figure 2.19

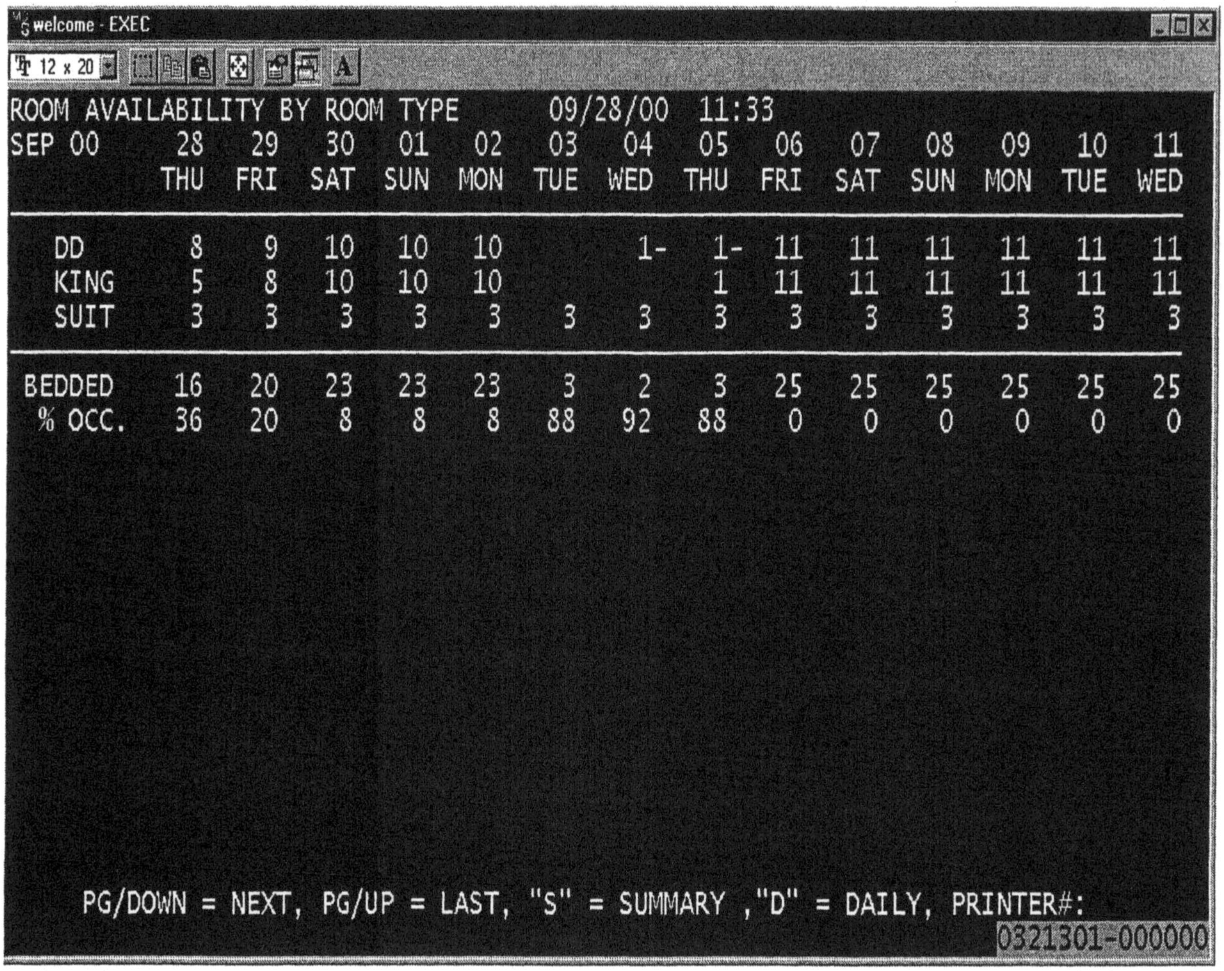

ROOM AVAILABILITY BY ROOM TYPE   09/28/00   11:33

SEP 00	28 THU	29 FRI	30 SAT	01 SUN	02 MON	03 TUE	04 WED	05 THU	06 FRI	07 SAT	08 SUN	09 MON	10 TUE	11 WED
DD	8	9	10	10	10		1-	1-	11	11	11	11	11	11
KING	5	8	10	10	10			1	11	11	11	11	11	11
SUIT	3	3	3	3	3	3	3	3	3	3	3	3	3	3
BEDDED	16	20	23	23	23	3	2	3	25	25	25	25	25	25
% OCC.	36	20	8	8	8	88	92	88	0	0	0	0	0	0

PG/DOWN = NEXT, PG/UP = LAST, "S" = SUMMARY ,"D" = DAILY, PRINTER#:

0321301-000000

Figure 2.20

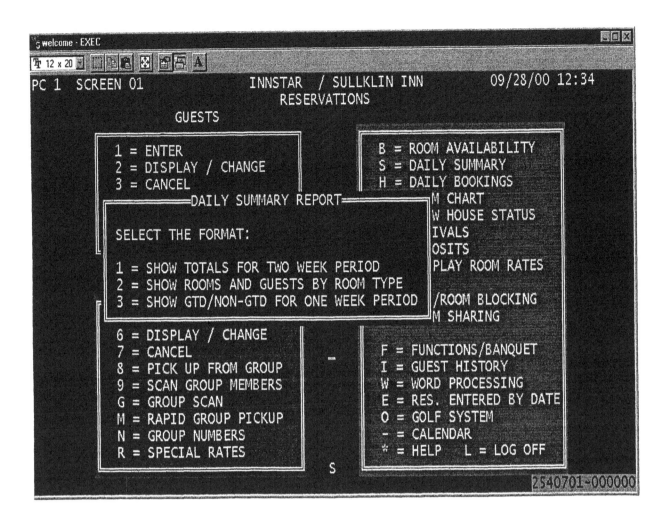

Figure 2.21

31

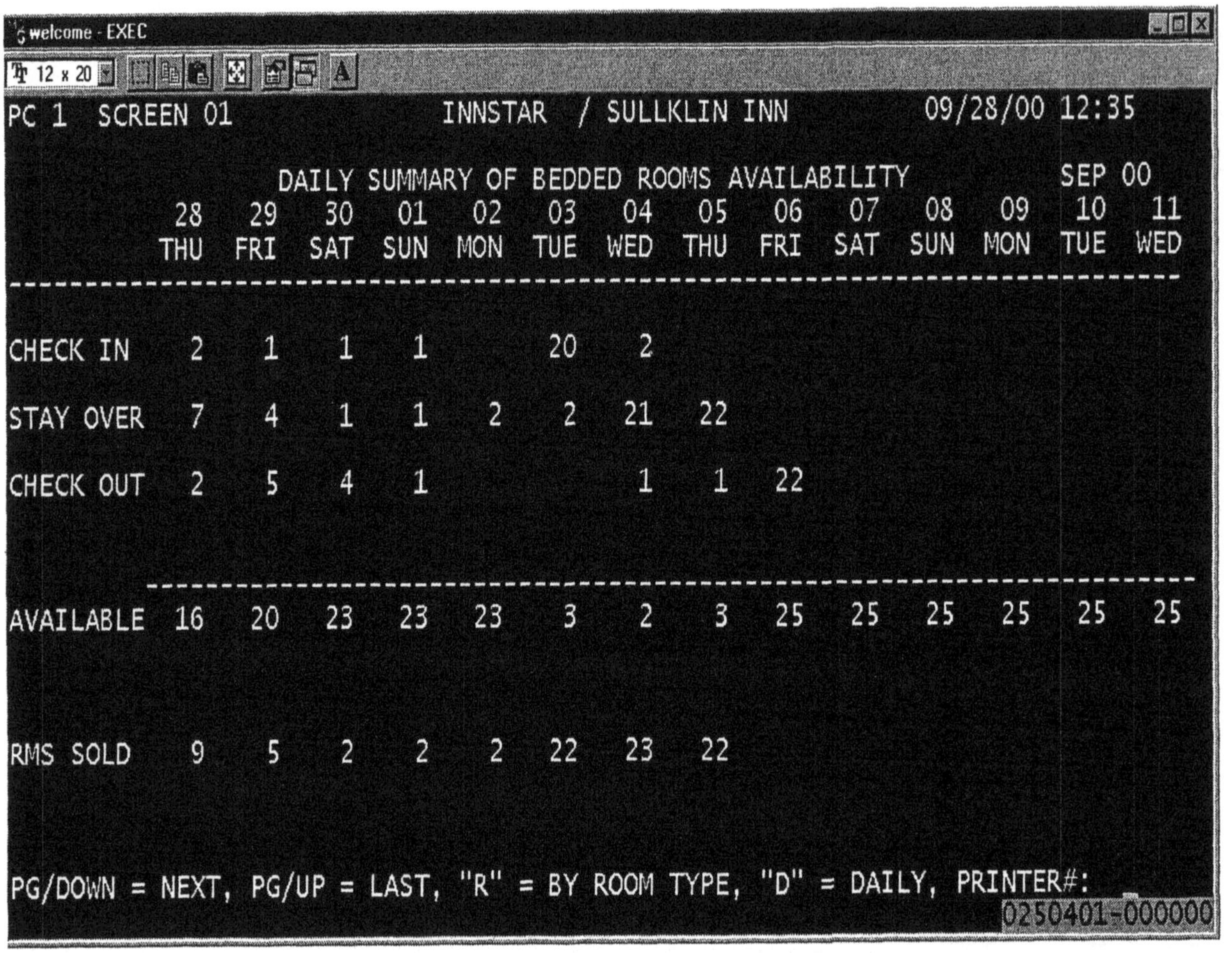

```
PC 1  SCREEN 01              INNSTAR  / SULLKLIN INN           09/28/00 12:35

              DAILY SUMMARY OF BEDDED ROOMS AVAILABILITY          SEP 00
         28    29    30    01    02    03    04    05    06    07    08    09    10    11
         THU   FRI   SAT   SUN   MON   TUE   WED   THU   FRI   SAT   SUN   MON   TUE   WED
-------------------------------------------------------------------------------------------

CHECK IN  2     1     1     1           20    2

STAY OVER 7     4     1     1     2     2     21    22

CHECK OUT 2     5     4     1                       1     1     22

          ---------------------------------------------------------------------------------
AVAILABLE 16    20    23    23    23    3     2     3     25    25    25    25    25    25


RMS SOLD  9     5     2     2     2     22    23    22


PG/DOWN = NEXT, PG/UP = LAST, "R" = BY ROOM TYPE, "D" = DAILY, PRINTER#:
                                                            0250401-000000
```

Figure 2.22

```
welcome - EXEC                                                              _ □ X
┌────────────────────────────────────────────────────────────────────────────┐
│ Tr 12 x 20 ▾  ▢▢▢ ▢ ▢▢ A                                                     │
├────────────────────────────────────────────────────────────────────────────┤
│ SULLKLIN INN              DAILY BOOKINGS   09/28/00  13:02                    │
│    DATE      AVAIL   GTD NGTD NPUP   OUT                                      │
│ 09/29/00 FR 020     001  000  000    000                                     │
│ 09/30/00 SA 023     000  001  000    000                                     │
│ 10/01/00 SU 023     001  000  000    000                                     │
│ 10/02/00 MO 023     000  000  000    000                                     │
│ 10/03/00 TU 003     002  018  018    000                                     │
│ 10/04/00 WE 002     002  000  000    000                                     │
│ 10/05/00 TH 003     000  000  000    000                                     │
│ 10/06/00 FR 025     000  000  000    000                                     │
│ 10/07/00 SA 025     000  000  000    000                                     │
│ 10/08/00 SU 025     000  000  000    000                                     │
│ 10/09/00 MO 025     000  000  000    000                                     │
│ 10/10/00 TU 025     000  000  000    000                                     │
│ 10/11/00 WE 025     000  000  000    000                                     │
│ 10/12/00 TH 025     000  000  000    000                                     │
│ 10/13/00 FR 025     000  000  000    000                                     │
│ 10/14/00 SA 024     001  000  000    000                                     │
│ 10/15/00 SU 024     000  000  000    000                                     │
│ 10/16/00 MO 024     000  000  000    000                                     │
│ 10/17/00 TU 024     000  000  000    000                                     │
│                                                                              │
│ NPUP = NOT PICKED-UP GROUP ROOMS    OUT = OUT OF ORDER ROOMS                  │
│ "R"=BY ROOM TYPE, "S"=SUMMARY, "PgDn" TO SEE NEXT 19 DAYS OR PRINTER #:       │
│                                                      0250401-000000           │
└────────────────────────────────────────────────────────────────────────────┘
```

Figure 2.23

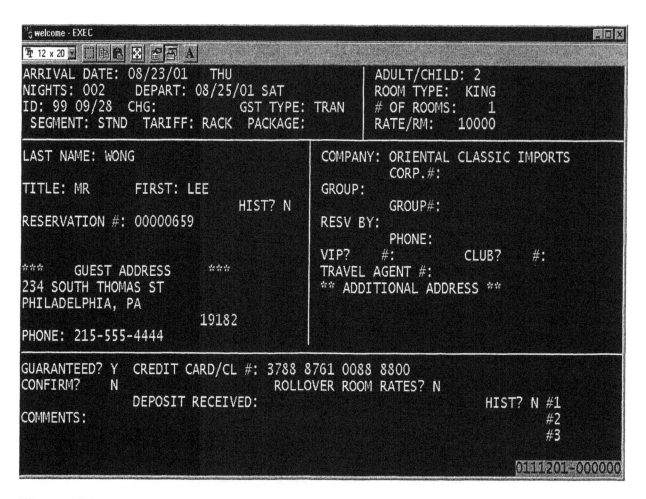

Figure 2.24

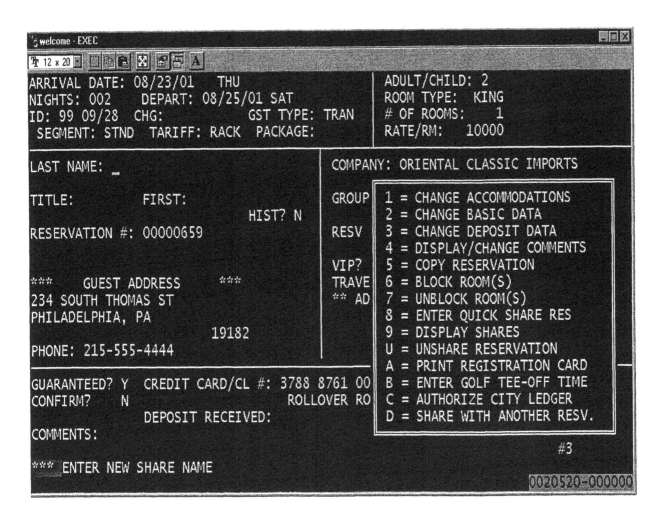

Figure 2.25

35

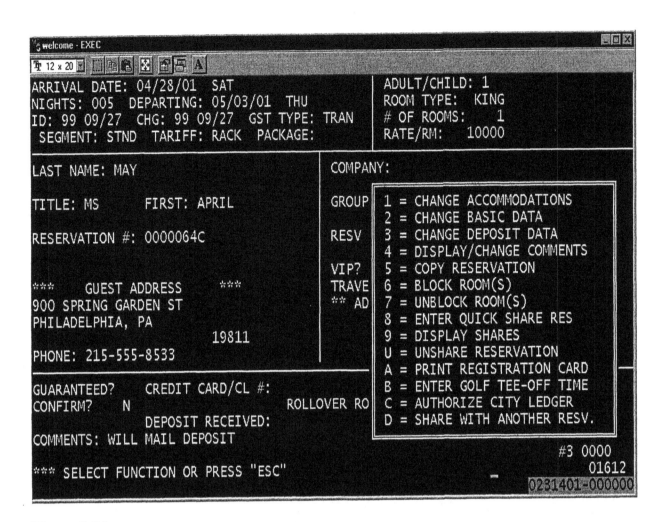

Figure 2.26

36

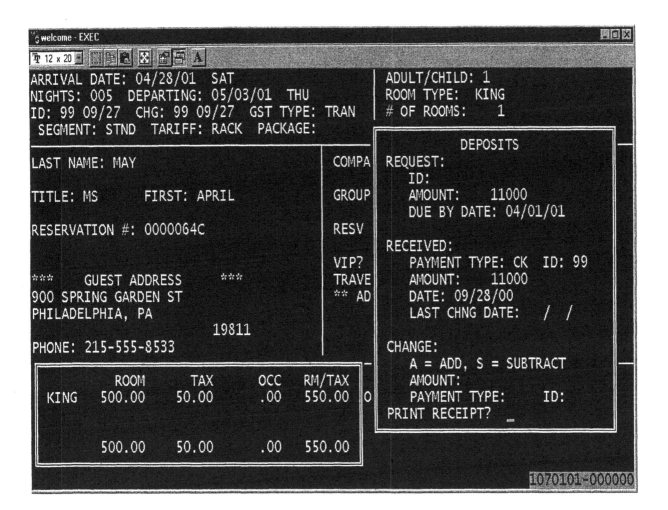

Figure 2.27

CHAPTER 3

REGISTRATION

Chapter Outline

Chapter 3 is all about the registration process. Guests are check in as walk-ins and with reservations. Each step in the registration process is discussed from the point the guest arrives at the hotel until they are given a room number and directed to a guestroom. Several special situations are also discussed. Students select rooms based upon room type and location. As you would find in an actual hotel the Sullklin Inn has three room types: king bed, double-double, and suite. Rooms offer views of the pool or park and smoking and non-smoking options.

Key Learning Concepts in Chapter 3
- How to register a guest with a reservation
- How to register a guest without a reservation (walk-in)
- How to find and change a reservation for a future date that arrives today
- What information is normally gathered at registration?
- Steps in a normal registration process

Additional Activities and Exercise Suggestions

1) Mr. John Wilson had a fire in his house. He and his family show up at the front desk with the clothes or their backs. He would like one Double Double room for his wife and two small children. He gives you a Discover card number, 6655 8585 9963 7535, and says he wants a room for 5 nights but may extend the number of nights to a longer length of stay due to the circumstances. His address is 49 County Line Rd, Pike PA 19113. Check the guests into the hotel.

    Answer: The students should check the guest and his family in and in the comment line state that the guest may want to extend his stay beyond the five nights. Also the hotel may want to do something to help the family and the student might mention some action like collecting toys for the children or clothing for the family.

2) Stu Tomatoe walked in from the parking lot. He says that he isn't sure if he needs a room for this evening and would like to find out some information. He says he prefers smoking room. How should you handle this situation?

    Answer: The students should check availability, after checking s/he will notice that there are double-double bedded smoking rooms available. At this point the student should encourage the man to make a reservation and provide him with the information about the room and rate.

3) Mr. Bob Bee of Barbee, PA, is at the front desk. He insists that he has a guaranteed reservation for one night and that he used his Master Card number 5551 8922 2225 3232 to

guarantee it. After searching for the reservation, none is found. It appears as if he did make a reservation but there is no record of it in the system. How should you handle this situation?

Answer: The student should check to see if the hotel has any rooms available. After finding a room the guest should be checked in using the credit card. The student should tell the guest that s/he will research the reservation and make sure that he was not charged for his original reservation record. It is possible that Mr. Bee had a reservation for the incorrect date and was charged as a no show. The student should advise Mr. Bee that if he has a charge on his card that is not related to this stay that he should contact the hotel to correct the charges.

Answers to Chapter 3 Exercises

1) The student finds his/her reservation in the reservation area of the computer by pressing R and typing in the first four letters of the student's last name. Then the student changes the arrival date from January 1, 2002, to September 28, 2000.

2) After the arrival date has been changed the student goes back to the main menu and pressing 1 for Check in W/Res. The reservation is checked into a suite. There are three suites and the room numbers are 300, 302, and 304.

3) a) When checking in a walk in the rooms appear and are listed with the comment pool or park. Also a student can go into S for Room Status scan and all rooms by the Pool are listed with the word pool next to the room number.

   b) Since the Tourmaline's are a married couple the student should put them in a king bedded room. If they do the room rate is $100 and the tax is $10. Therefore, the student should collect $110 at check in. A minimum of payment in full is collected for all cash customers.

4) a) Check room availability to ensure that there is a room available to walk in a guest. The student should look up the reservation for Mr. Nelson for arrival date September 29. Then the student changes the arrival date for today, September 28. Now the guest is checked in using 1 from the main menu for Check in with a reservation. During the check in the process the student needs to check that the number of nights stay is correct.

5) a) What room rate did you give Mr. Murky? This depends on the room type. The room rate for a Double Double is $75 for a King is $90 and for a suite it is $190. The student checks Mr. Murky in as a Walk-In Guest by pressing 2 from the main menu.

6) a) Depending on how the students assigned rooms at check-in the previous examples there may not be a king room available. If no king room is available, the student should offer the guest a Double Double-bedded room. The student should not insist upon a phone number and take the Visa card number at check in. The assumption is that he is staying one night.

7) There should be nine rooms available. Most likely the student will have 6 Double Double, 1 King and 2 Suites available. However, the student may have assigned rooms differently than in the examples so their availability by room type may vary from the example.

8) 64%. This is an acceptable level of occupancy, it is not low but it is not considered very high.

Transparency Masters for the Chapter 3 Workbook figures can be found beginning the next page.

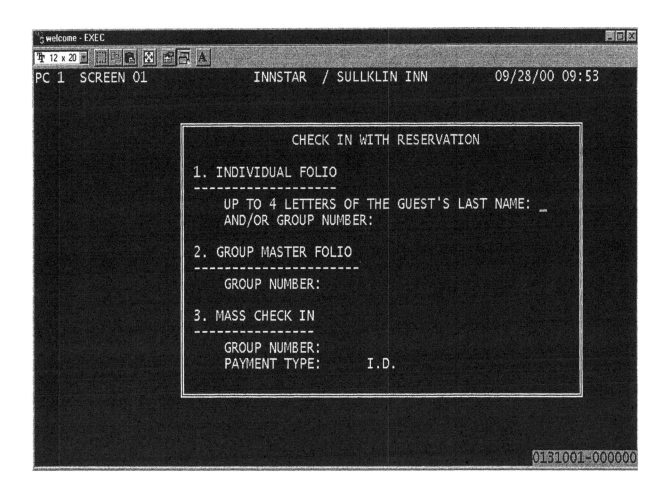

Figure 3.1

41

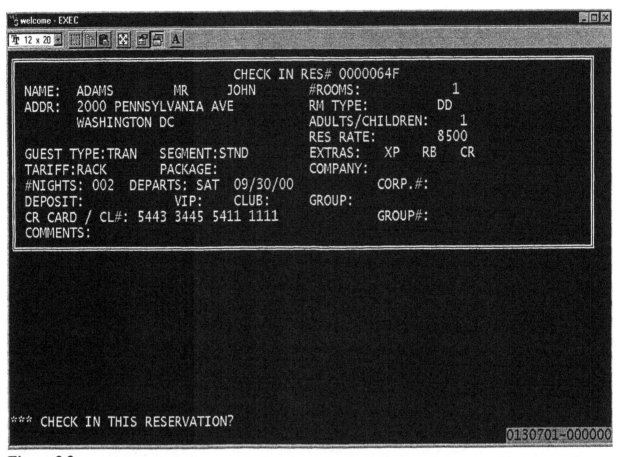

Figure 3.2

42

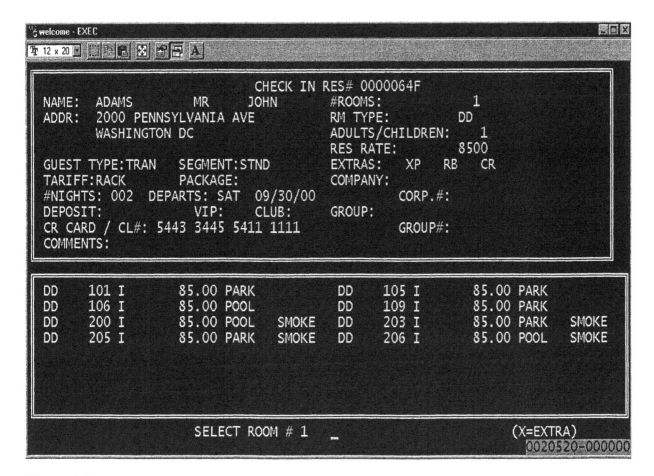

Figure 3.3

43

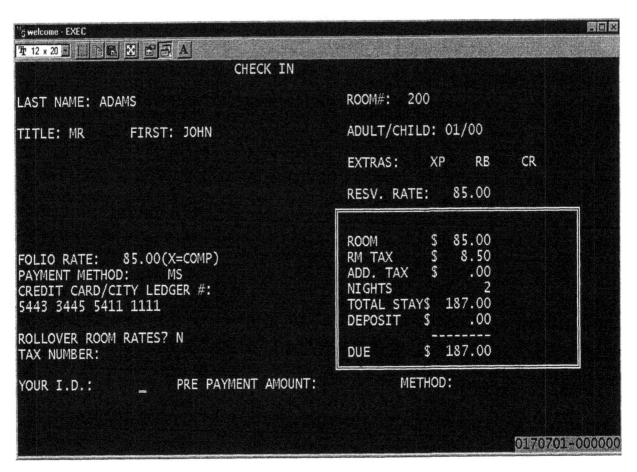

Figure 3.4

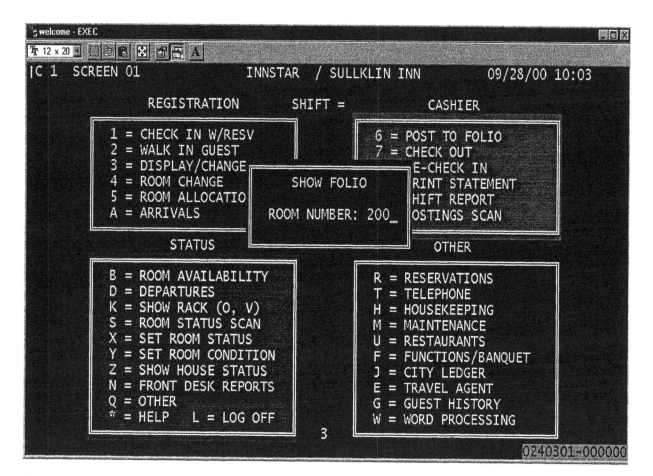

Figure 3.5

45

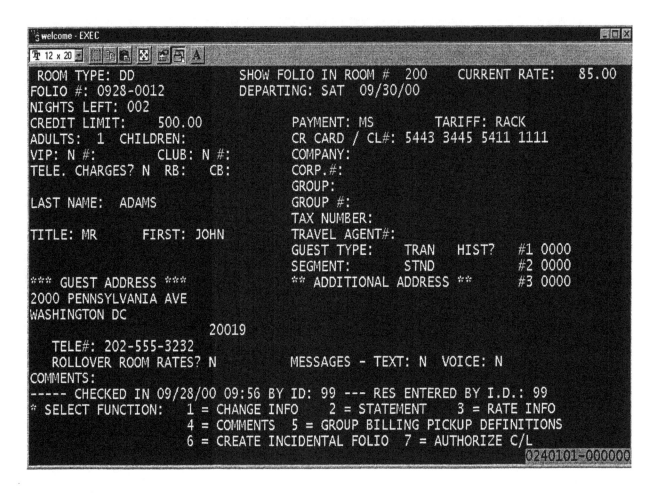

Figure 3.6

46

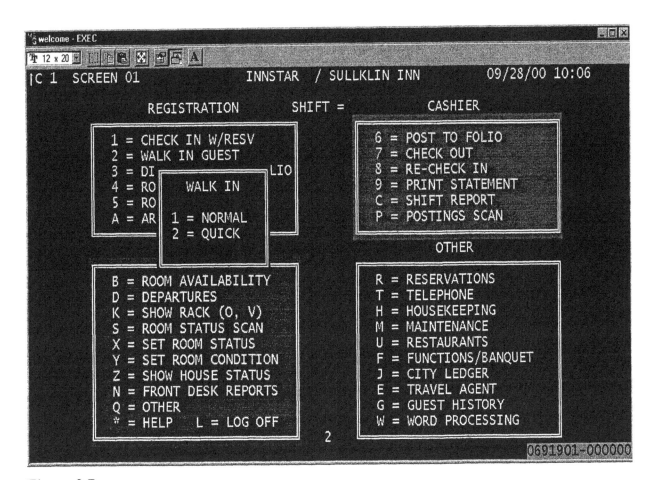

Figure 3.7

47

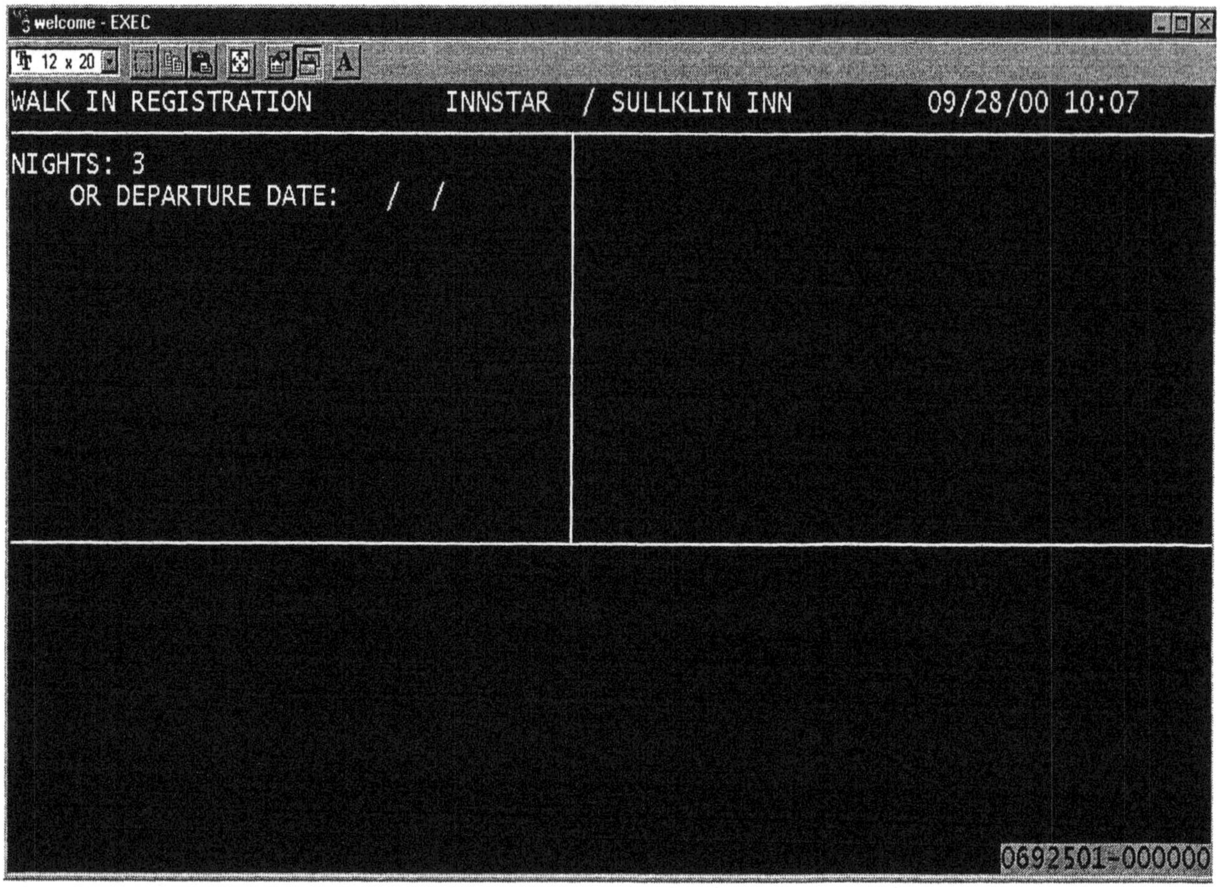

Figure 3.8

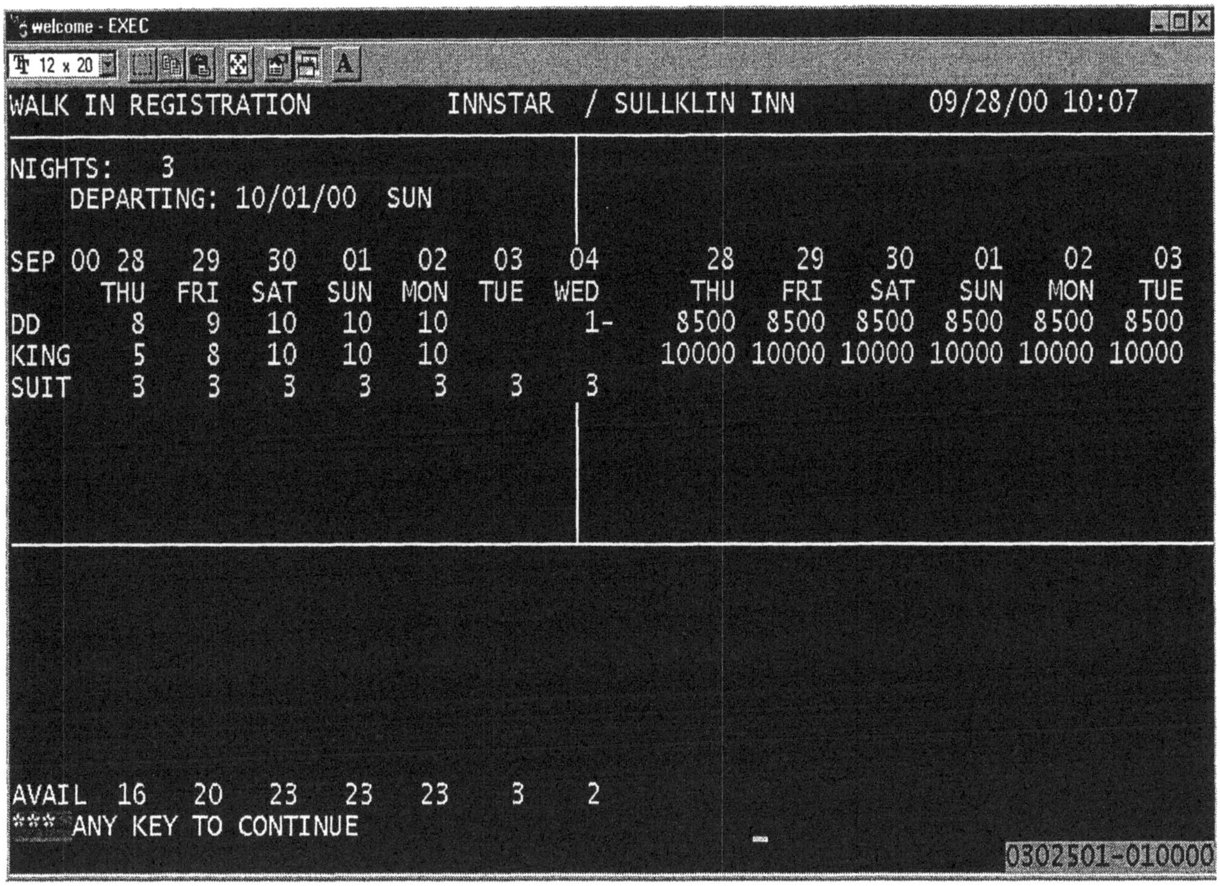
welcome - EXEC
12 x 20
WALK IN REGISTRATION INNSTAR / SULLKLIN INN 09/28/00 10:07
NIGHTS: 3
DEPARTING: 10/01/00 SUN
SEP 00 28 29 30 01 02 03 04 28 29 30 01 02 03
THU FRI SAT SUN MON TUE WED THU FRI SAT SUN MON TUE
DD 8 9 10 10 10 1- 8500 8500 8500 8500 8500 8500
KING 5 8 10 10 10 10000 10000 10000 10000 10000 10000
SUIT 3 3 3 3 3 3 3
AVAIL 16 20 23 23 23 3 2
*** ANY KEY TO CONTINUE
0302501-010000

Figure 3.9

```
welcome - EXEC

[Tr 12 x 20]  [toolbar icons] A

WALK IN REGISTRATION        INNSTAR / SULLKLIN INN        09/28/00 10:10

NIGHTS:  3                         ADULTS:    CHILDREN:
    DEPARTING: 10/01/00  SUN       EXTRAS:  XP   RB   CR
LAST NAME:                         COMPANY:
TITLE:       FIRST:                         CORP.#:
             SEARCH HISTORY? N     GROUP:
GUEST TYPE:     SEGMENT:                    GROUP#:
TARIFF:         PACKAGE:
***    GUEST ADDRESS      ***      ** ADDITIONAL ADDRESS **




PHONE:   -                         VIP?  #:      CLUB?  #:

COMMENTS:






                                                  0020520-000000
```

Figure 3.10

50

```
welcome - EXEC                                                          [_][□][X]
T 12 x 20 [icons] A

WALK IN REGISTRATION        INNSTAR  / SULLKLIN INN          09/28/00 11:03

NIGHTS:   3                        ADULTS: 1   CHILDREN:
    DEPARTING: 10/01/00  SUN       EXTRAS:  XP   RB   CR
LAST NAME: TANAKA                  COMPANY:
TITLE: MS       FIRST: YUKI                  CORP.#:
                SEARCH HISTORY? N  GROUP:
GUEST TYPE: TRAN  SEGMENT: STND              GROUP#:
TARIFF: RACK       PACKAGE:
***      GUEST ADDRESS      ***    ** ADDITIONAL ADDRESS **
7 LUCKY DRIVE
ATLANTIC CITY NJ
DD     101 I      85.00 PARK       KING   102 I     100.00 POOL
DD     105 I      85.00 PARK       DD     106 I      85.00 POOL
KING   107 I     100.00 PARK       DD     109 I      85.00 PARK
DD     203 I      85.00 PARK SMOKE DD     205 I      85.00 PARK  SMOKE
DD     206 I      85.00 POOL SMOKE KING   207 I     100.00 PARK  SMOKE
SUIT   300 I            PARK       KING   301 I     100.00 POOL
SUIT   302 I            PARK       SUIT   304 I            PARK
KING   303 D     100.00 POOL


                    SELECT ROOM # 1
                                                    0302601-000100
```

Figure 3.11

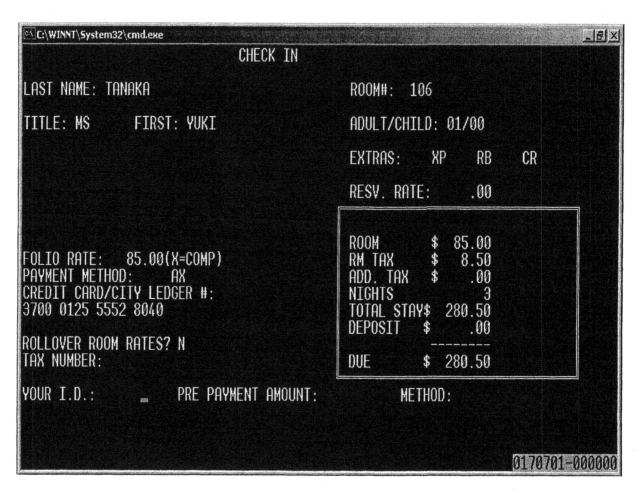

Figure 3.12

```
C:\WINNT\System32\cmd.exe                                        _ B X

 ROOM TYPE: DD          SHOW FOLIO IN ROOM #  106   CURRENT RATE:   85.00
FOLIO #: 0928-0012      DEPARTING: SUN  10/01/00
NIGHTS LEFT: 003
CREDIT LIMIT:    500.00          PAYMENT: AX        TARIFF: RACK
ADULTS:  1  CHILDREN:            CR CARD / CL#: 3700 0125 5552 8040
VIP: N #:        CLUB: N #:      COMPANY:
TELE. CHARGES? N  RB:   CB:      CORP.#:
                                 GROUP:
LAST NAME:  TANAKA               GROUP #:
                                 TAX NUMBER:
TITLE: MS       FIRST: YUKI      TRAVEL AGENT#:
                                 GUEST TYPE:    TRAN   HIST?   #1 0000
                                 SEGMENT:       STND           #2 0000
*** GUEST ADDRESS ***            ** ADDITIONAL ADDRESS **      #3 0000
7 LUCKY DRIVE
ATLANTIC CITY NJ
                    08401
   TELE#: 609-555-8888
   ROLLOVER ROOM RATES? N        MESSAGES - TEXT: N  VOICE: N
COMMENTS:
----- CHECKED IN 09/28/00 16:30 BY ID: 99 --- WALK IN
* SELECT FUNCTION: _ 1 = CHANGE INFO   2 = STATEMENT   3 = RATE INFO
               4 = COMMENTS  5 = GROUP BILLING PICKUP DEFINITIONS
               6 = CREATE INCIDENTAL FOLIO  7 = AUTHORIZE C/L
                                                    0241001-000000
```

Figure 3.13

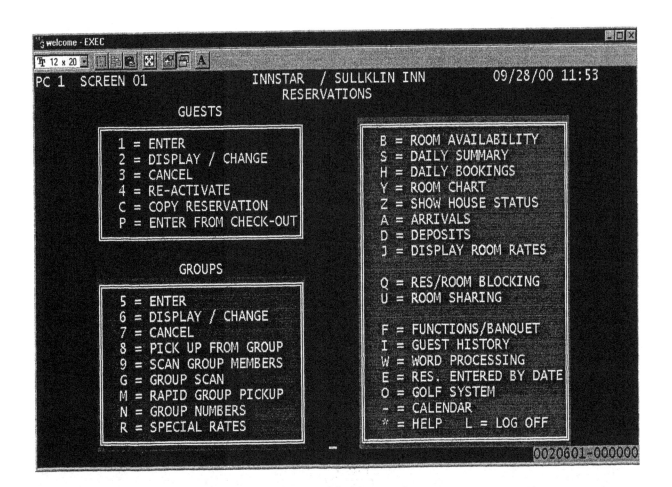

Figure 3.14

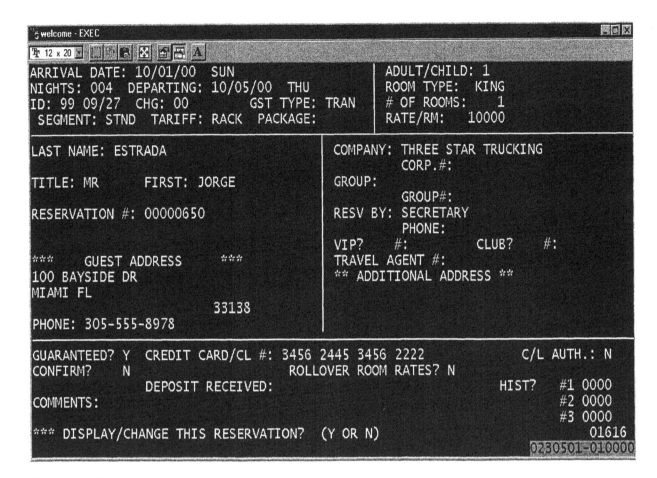

Figure 3.15

55

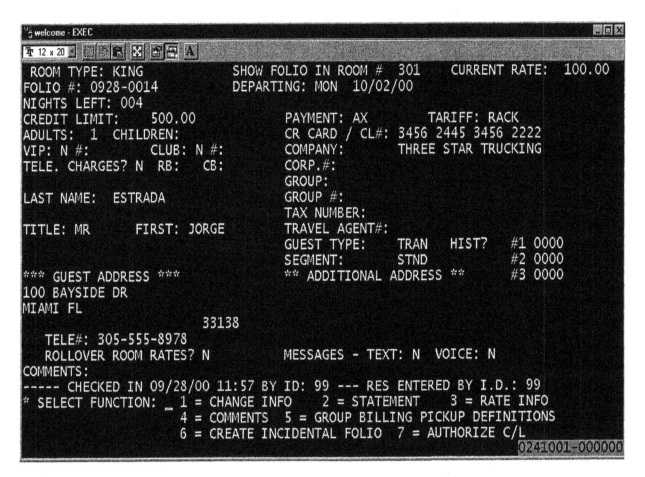

Figure 3.16

56

CHAPTER 4

POSTING AND FOLIO MANAGEMENT

Chapter Outline

Posting and folio management is covered in Chapter 4. The cashier functions include posting a variety of payments and charges. Debits and credits are explored in this chapter. Students also make posting corrections and transfer charges. This chapter includes the steps in a check-out process and the creation of the cashier end of shift report. The posting functions of this property management system are fully explored.

Key Learning Concepts in Chapter 4
- Posting to a folio directly from PM
- Posting to a folio via an interface
- Correction to a posting
- Transfer of a posting
- Check-out
- Cashier end of shift reporting

Additional Activities and Exercise Suggestions

1) Post the following charges to Mr. Graw's room. A $5.00 fax charge and a $9.00 movie charge.

2) Room 100 makes three long distance phone calls to Wilmington, DE. Each call is $1.00 and the corresponding reference numbers are 03, 04, 05. Mr. Sullivan calls the front desk and says that only two of the phone calls went through. He agrees to pay for 2 calls but not 3. How would you handle this situation?

3) Mr. Eubuzzoffsky would like to tip the food server in the restaurant. He needs $5.00 and you give him a $5.00 paid out. Enter this transaction in the system.

Answers to Chapter 4 Exercises

1) Each phone call should be posted separately using separate reference numbers.

2) Room, Tax, Local Telephone call, Long distance telephone call, Fax, Movie, Room Account, Refund, Paid out

3) Cash, Check, American Express, Visa, Master Card, Discover, D/B, and Room Account

4) $15.00; Enter 6 from the Main Menu for Post to Folio, then enter the room number 103. Then press 1 for new posting ant he minus symbol for posting a credit. Type 80 for cash and enter the amount of the call.

5) Enter 6 from the Main Menu for Post to Folio, then enter the room number 202. Since this is a correction enter 2 to make a correction. Enter a minus symbol to post a credit. Find the number that corresponds to the duplicate movie charge. The number is 4 some students may enter 3 and this acceptable. Enter the number 4 and then enter the amount of the movie charge, $9.00. The comment should say that this is a duplicate charge. The student completes the transaction by entering his/ her ID number.

6) Enter 6 from the Main Menu for Post to Folio, then enter the room number 108 and then press 4 for Transferring one posting. Now press the plus symbol and then 3, the number corresponding to the charge that you would like to transfer. Enter the full amount of the charge $18.00. Complete the transaction by entering the correct room number 103 and the student's ID number.

7) Enter 7 for Check out and then the room number 202. Ask the guest if she had a nice stay. Then confirm all the charges on the folio to ensure that it is correct. Ask the guest if she had any other recent charges. Confirm the use of her American Express card and enter the student's ID number. Select N for no guest history. Continue to press enter and process the check out. Thank the guest for staying at the Sullklin Inn and wish her a good trip home.

8) Opening balance $_____$500_____
   Cash $_____
   Check $_____
   List any credit card receipts $_____
   Closing balance $_____
These numbers may vary depending upon the student's previous homework assignments.

Transparency Masters for the Chapter 4 Workbook figures can be found beginning the next page.

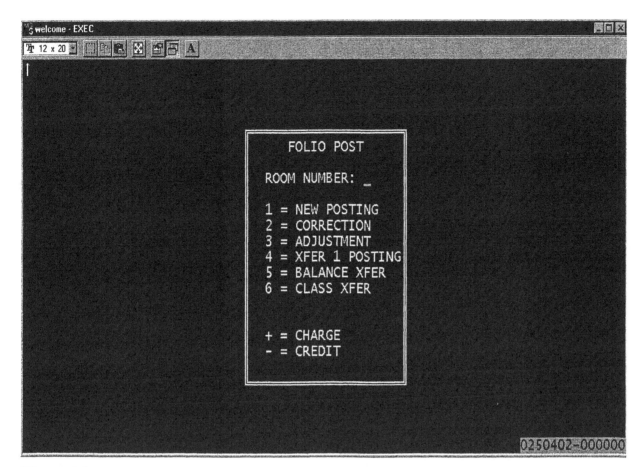

Figure 4.1

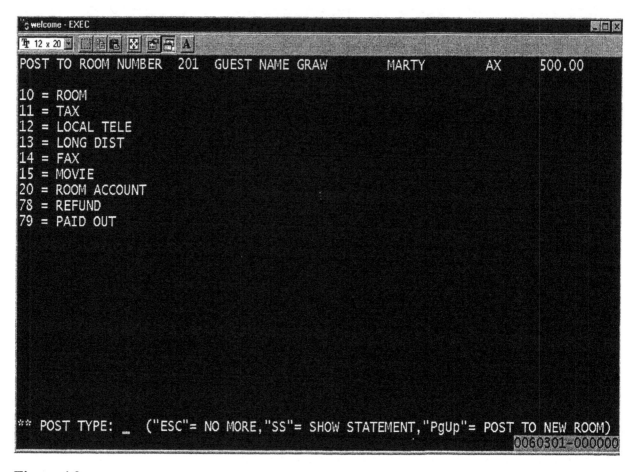

Figure 4.2

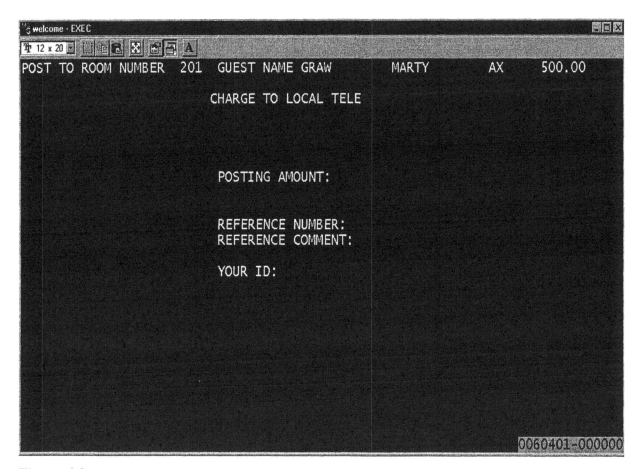

Figure 4.3

```
welcome - EXEC                                                    _ □ ✕
Tr 12 x 20 ▾  ▯ ▣ ▣ ▣ ▣ ▣ A
POST TO ROOM NUMBER  201   GUEST NAME GRAW        MARTY      AX      500.00

10 = ROOM
11 = TAX
12 = LOCAL TELE
13 = LONG DIST
14 = FAX
15 = MOVIE
20 = ROOM ACCOUNT
78 = REFUND
79 = PAID OUT















**** POST DONE!
** POST TYPE:      ("ESC"= NO MORE,"SS"= SHOW STATEMENT,"PgUp"= POST TO NEW ROOM)
                                                     1030101-000100
```

Figure 4.4

62

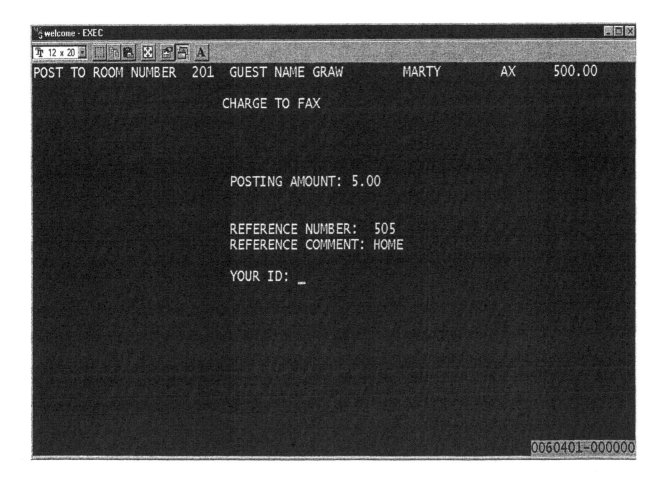

Figure 4.5

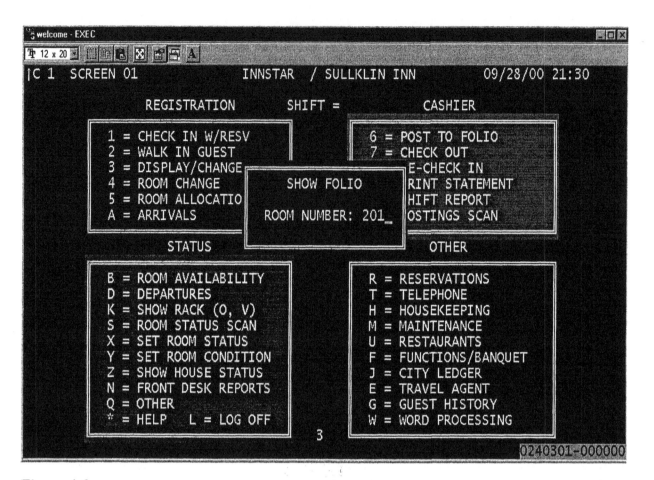

Figure 4.6

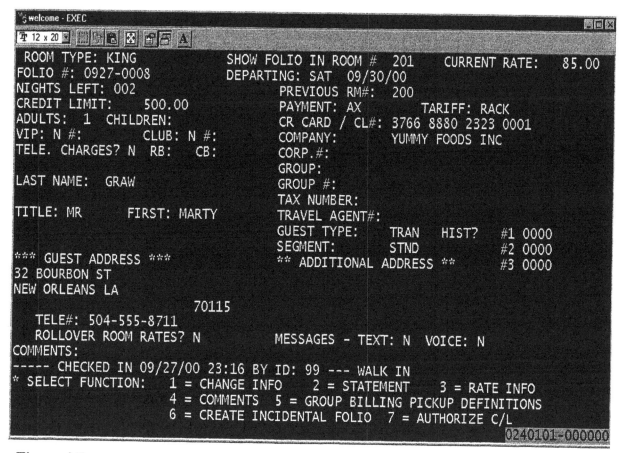

Figure 4.7

65

```
┌─────────────────────────────────────────────────────────────────────────┐
│ ᴹꜱ welcome - EXEC                                                _ □ X     │
├─────────────────────────────────────────────────────────────────────────┤
│ 🔠 12 x 20 ▾ 🗆🗅🗔 🗙 🗇🗗 A                                                  │
├─────────────────────────────────────────────────────────────────────────┤
│                            STATEMENT                                       │
│ ROOM:  201   GUEST: GRAW         PAY METHOD & LIMIT: AX   500.00  PERS: 01 │
│                                                                            │
│ NO.   DATE       REF    DESCRIPTION      COMMENT        AMOUNT     ID       │
│ ────────────────────────────────────────────────────────────────────────│
│  1.  09/27         1    ROOM                             85.00   SYSTEM     │
│  2.  09/27              TAX                               8.50   SYSTEM     │
│  3.  09/28       123    LOCAL TELE       LOCAL            1.20    99         │
│  4.  09/28       505    FAX              HOME            5.00    99         │
│                         *** BALANCE ***                 99.70              │
│                                                                            │
│                                                                            │
│                                                                            │
│                                                                            │
│                                                                            │
│                                                                            │
│                                                                            │
│                                                                            │
│                                                                            │
│ **** (SPACE = CONTINUE)  or PgUp for Prev Page                            │
│                                                             0640101-000000 │
└─────────────────────────────────────────────────────────────────────────┘
```

Figure 4.8

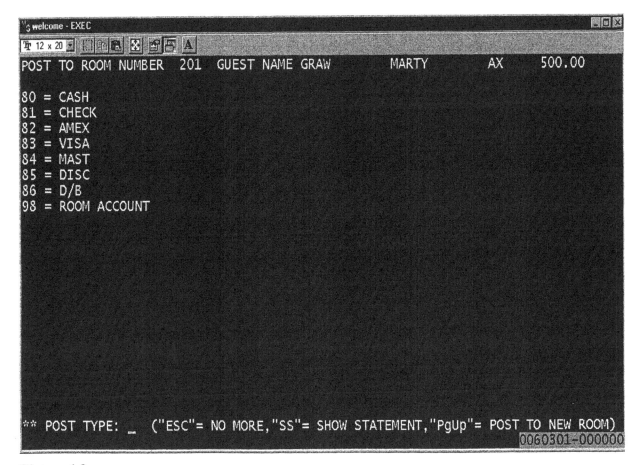

Figure 4.9

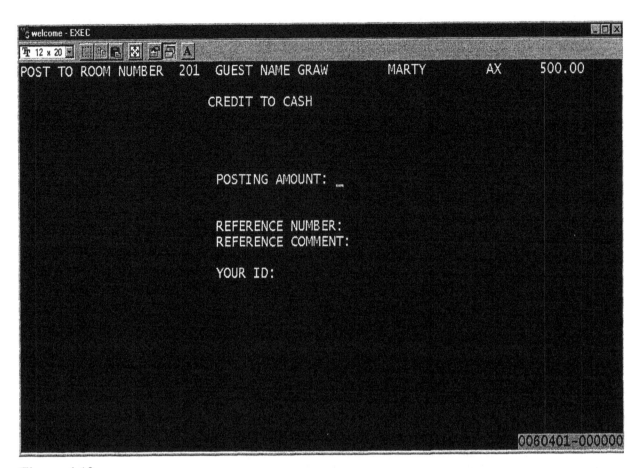

Figure 4.10

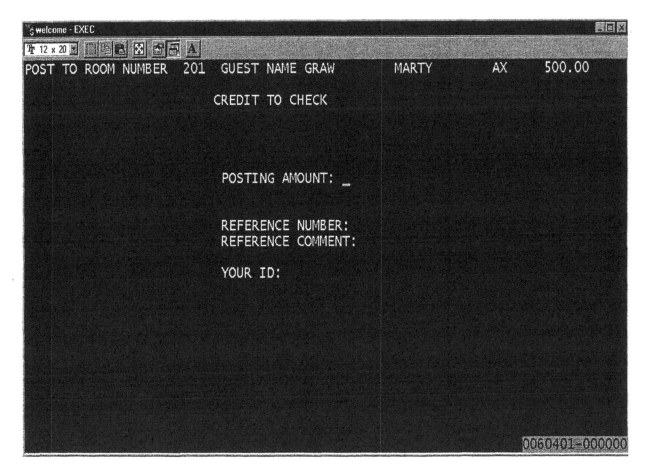

Figure 4.11

```
welcome - EXEC                                                              [_][□][X]
Tr 12 x 20 ▼  [::][▣][▣] [▨] [▣][▤] [A]
                                 STATEMENT
ROOM:  201   GUEST: GRAW         PAY METHOD & LIMIT: AX   500.00   PERS: 01

NO.   DATE      REF    DESCRIPTION       COMMENT        AMOUNT      ID

 1.   09/27       1    ROOM                              85.00     SYSTEM
 2.   09/27            TAX                                8.50     SYSTEM
 3.   09/28     123    LOCAL TELE        LOCAL            1.20     99
 4.   09/28     505    FAX               HOME             5.00     99
 5.   09/28     201    CASH              CASH          100.00CR    99
 6.   09/28     101    CHECK             CHECK 16       50.00CR    99
                        ***  BALANCE  ***               50.30CR




**** (SPACE = CONTINUE)   or PgUp for Prev Page
                                                        0640101-000000
```

Figure 4.12

70

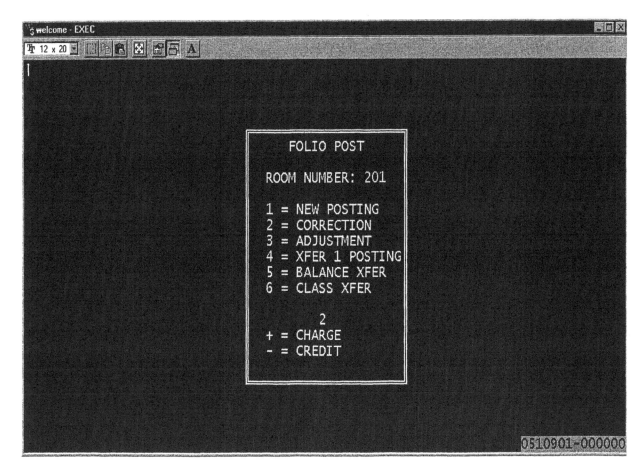

Figure 4.13

71

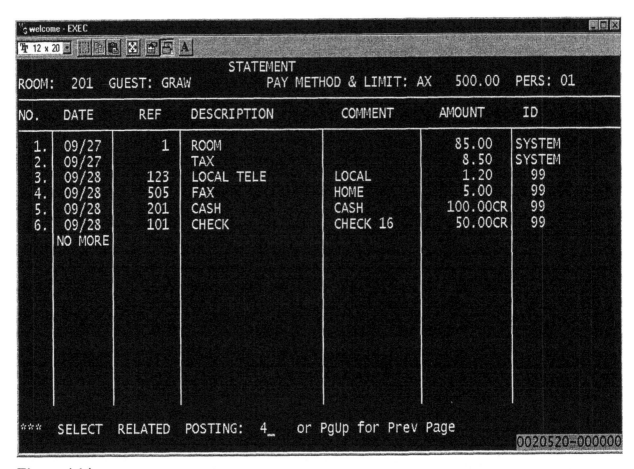

Figure 4.14

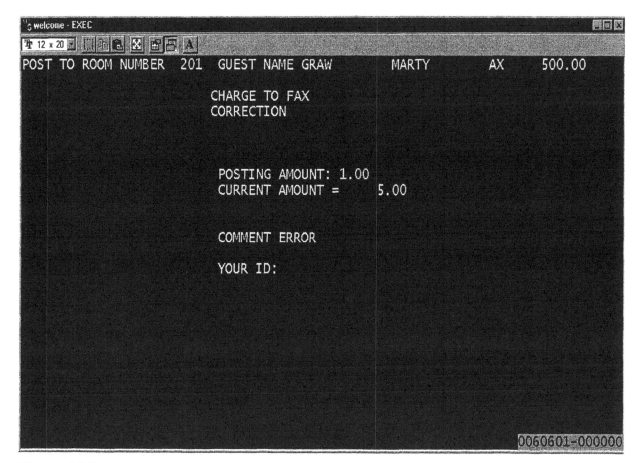

Figure 4.15

```
welcome - EXEC                                                              _ □ ☒
[T 12 x 20 ▼] [▯][▯][▯] [☒][▯][▯] [A]
                            STATEMENT
ROOM:  201  GUEST: GRAW         PAY METHOD & LIMIT: AX   500.00   PERS: 01

NO.   DATE      REF    DESCRIPTION         COMMENT        AMOUNT      ID

 1.  09/27        1    ROOM                                85.00   SYSTEM
 2.  09/27             TAX                                  8.50   SYSTEM
 3.  09/28      123    LOCAL TELE          LOCAL            1.20   99
 4.  09/28      505    FAX                 HOME             5.00   99
 5.  09/28      201    CASH                CASH         100.00CR   99
 6.  09/28      101    CHECK               CHECK 16      50.00CR   99
 7.  09/28      505    FAX         CORR    ERROR            1.00   99
                        *** BALANCE ***                  49.30CR




**** (SPACE = CONTINUE)  or PgUp for Prev Page
                                                      0640101-000000
```

Figure 4.16

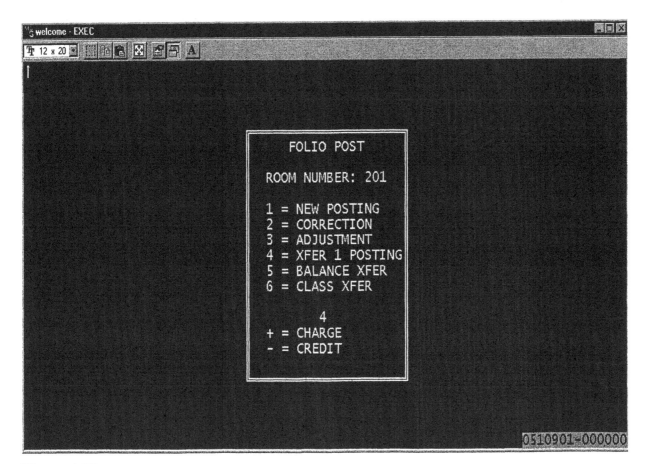

Figure 4.17

```
welcome - EXEC                                                          ☐▣✕
T 12 x 20 ▼ ▣▣▣▣▣▣ A
                              STATEMENT
ROOM:  201  GUEST: GRAW           PAY METHOD & LIMIT: AX   500.00  PERS: 01

NO.   DATE      REF   DESCRIPTION      COMMENT        AMOUNT     ID

  1.  09/27       1   ROOM                             85.00  SYSTEM
  2.  09/27           TAX                               8.50  SYSTEM
  3.  09/28     123   LOCAL TELE       LOCAL            1.20  99
  4.  09/28     505   FAX              HOME             5.00  99
  5.  09/28     201   CASH             CASH         100.00CR  99
  6.  09/28     101   CHECK            CHECK 16      50.00CR  99
      NO MORE










SELECT RELATED POSTING: 3   (PgUp for Prev Page) ENTER AMOUNT IF PARTIAL:
                                                    0020520-000000
```

Figure 4.18

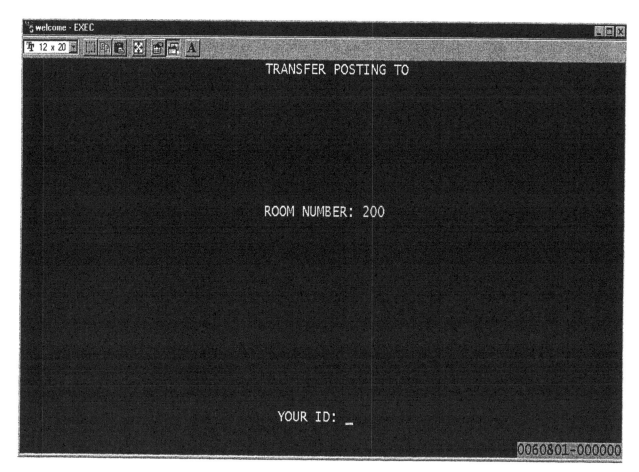

Figure 4.19

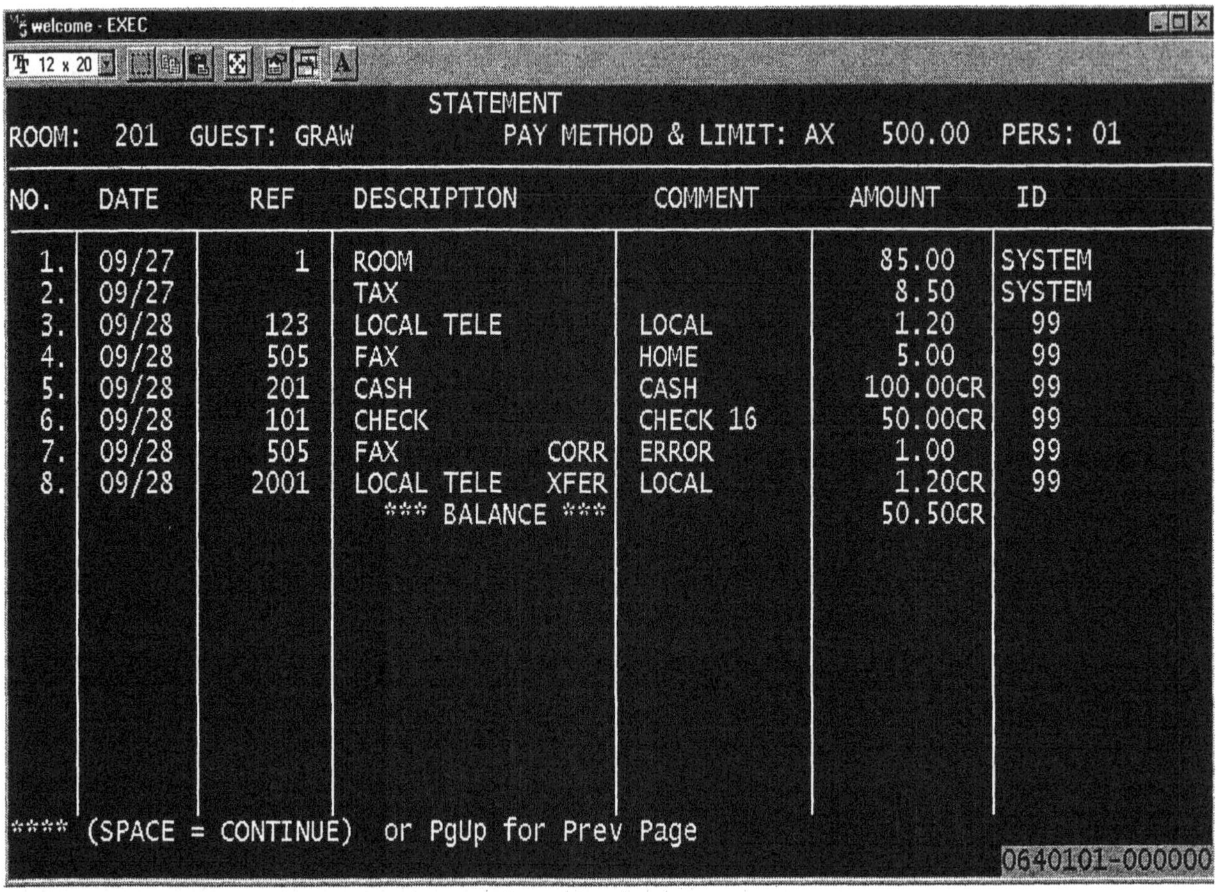

```
welcome - EXEC                                                      [_][□][X]

[T 12 x 20 ▾] [□][▦][▣][▤][▥][▦][A]

                              STATEMENT
ROOM:  201  GUEST: GRAW         PAY METHOD & LIMIT: AX   500.00  PERS: 01

NO.  DATE     REF    DESCRIPTION       COMMENT      AMOUNT      ID

 1.  09/27      1    ROOM                            85.00    SYSTEM
 2.  09/27           TAX                              8.50    SYSTEM
 3.  09/28    123    LOCAL TELE        LOCAL          1.20    99
 4.  09/28    505    FAX               HOME           5.00    99
 5.  09/28    201    CASH              CASH        100.00CR    99
 6.  09/28    101    CHECK             CHECK 16     50.00CR    99
 7.  09/28    505    FAX        CORR   ERROR          1.00    99
 8.  09/28   2001    LOCAL TELE  XFER  LOCAL          1.20CR   99
                     *** BALANCE ***                50.50CR


**** (SPACE = CONTINUE)  or PgUp for Prev Page
                                                    0640101-000000
```

Figure 4.20

78

```
welcome - EXEC                                                    [_][□][X]
┌─────────────────────────────────────────────────────────────────────────┐
│ Tr 12 x 20 ▾  [□][▣][▪][▩][▩][▤][A]                                        │
├───────────────────────────────────────────────────────────────────────────┤
│                            STATEMENT                                        │
│ ROOM:  201  GUEST: GRAW         PAY METHOD & LIMIT: AX   500.00  PERS: 01   │
├───────────────────────────────────────────────────────────────────────────┤
│ NO.   DATE      REF     DESCRIPTION        COMMENT      AMOUNT      ID       │
│                                                                             │
│  1.  09/27       1      ROOM                            85.00     SYSTEM     │
│  2.  09/27              TAX                              8.50     SYSTEM     │
│  3.  09/28      123     LOCAL TELE         LOCAL         1.20      99        │
│  4.  09/28      505     FAX                HOME          5.00      99        │
│  5.  09/28      201     CASH               CASH       100.00CR     99        │
│  6.  09/28      101     CHECK              CHECK 16    50.00CR      99        │
│  7.  09/28      505     FAX         CORR   ERROR         1.00      99        │
│  8.  09/28      2001    LOCAL TELE  XFER   LOCAL         1.20CR     99        │
│                       *** BALANCE ***                  50.50CR               │
│                                                                             │
│                                                                             │
│                                                                             │
│                                                                             │
│                                                                             │
│                                                                             │
│                                                                             │
│ **** (SPACE = CONTINUE)   or PgUp for Prev Page                             │
│                                                           0640101-000000    │
└─────────────────────────────────────────────────────────────────────────┘
```

Figure 4.21

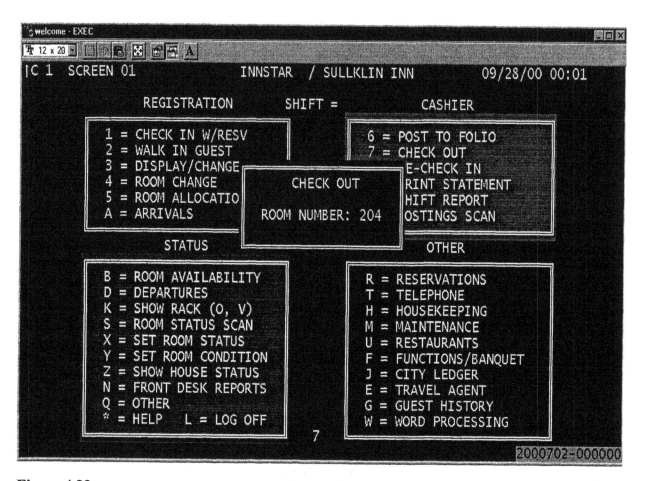

Figure 4.22

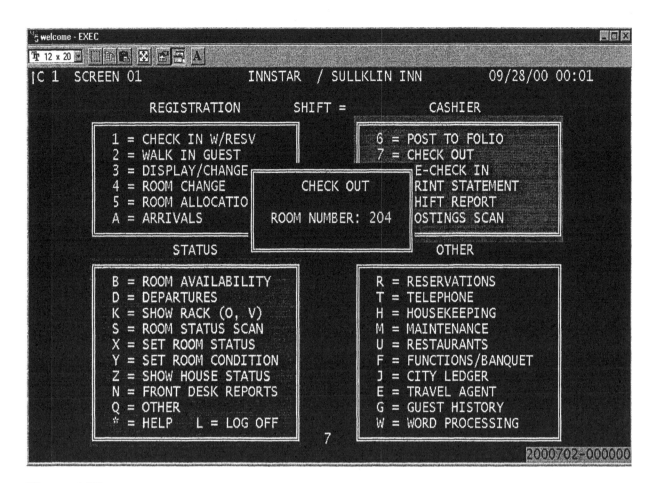

Figure 4.23

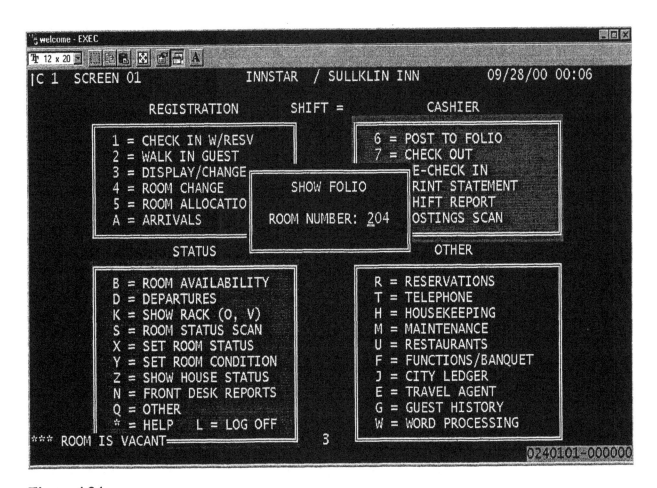

Figure 4.24

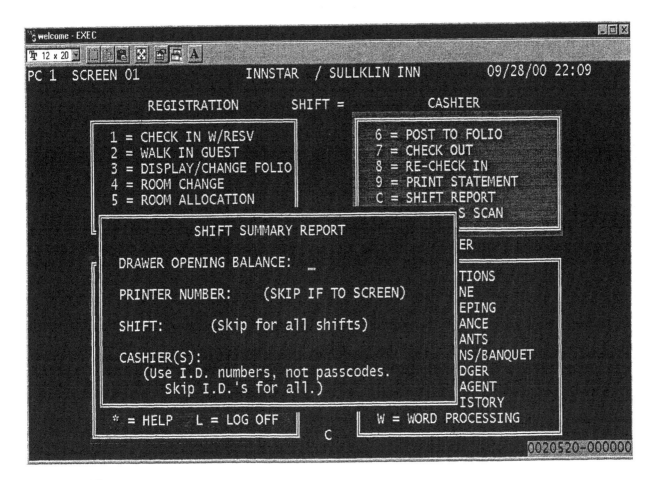

Figure 4.25

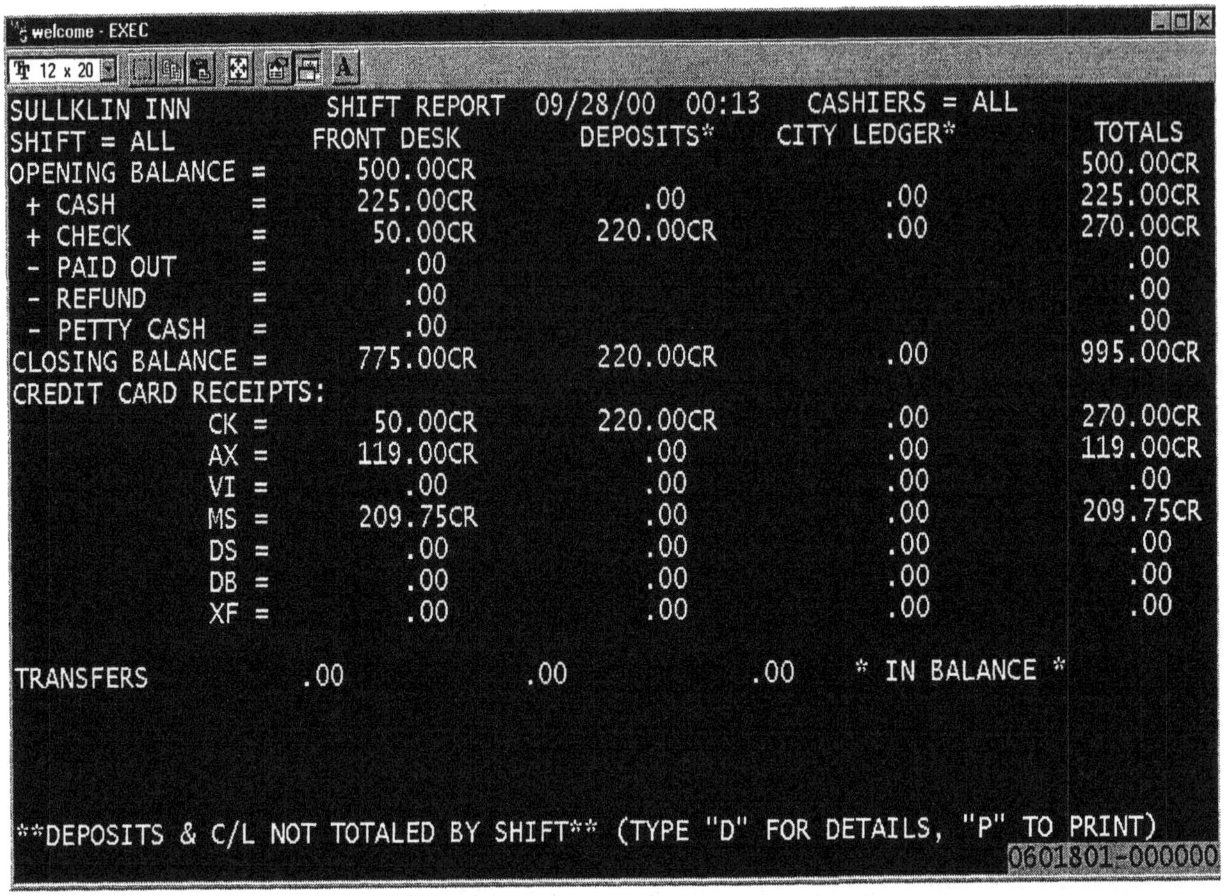

```
welcome - EXEC                                                              _ □ ×
T 12 x 20 ▯ ▯▯▯▯ ▯▯A

SULLKLIN INN           SHIFT REPORT  09/28/00  00:13   CASHIERS = ALL
SHIFT = ALL            FRONT DESK       DEPOSITS*      CITY LEDGER*          TOTALS
OPENING BALANCE =        500.00CR                                          500.00CR
 + CASH         =        225.00CR           .00            .00             225.00CR
 + CHECK        =         50.00CR        220.00CR          .00             270.00CR
 - PAID OUT     =           .00                                               .00
 - REFUND       =           .00                                               .00
 - PETTY CASH   =           .00                                               .00
CLOSING BALANCE =        775.00CR        220.00CR          .00             995.00CR
CREDIT CARD RECEIPTS:
           CK =           50.00CR        220.00CR          .00             270.00CR
           AX =          119.00CR           .00           .00             119.00CR
           VI =             .00             .00           .00                .00
           MS =          209.75CR           .00           .00             209.75CR
           DS =             .00             .00           .00                .00
           DB =             .00             .00           .00                .00
           XF =             .00             .00           .00                .00


TRANSFERS              .00             .00             .00    *  IN BALANCE  *




**DEPOSITS & C/L NOT TOTALED BY SHIFT** (TYPE "D" FOR DETAILS, "P" TO PRINT)
                                                          0601801-000000
```

Figure 4.26

84

CHAPTER 5

GUEST SERVICES

Chapter Outline

Chapter 5 involves two important hotel departments and how they interface with the front desk. The housekeeping functions and maintenance functions are used in this chapter to demonstrate their impact on the operation of the front desk. The telephone department and PBX functions are also explored. Students change room status and conditions for hotel rooms. Maintenance work orders are handled and telephone messages are taken in this chapter.

Key Learning Concepts in Chapter 5

Housekeeping
- Room Status
- Room Condition
Maintenance
- Work Orders
Telephone
- Message Services
- Guest Search

Additional Activities and Exercise Suggestions

1) Mr. Levy in room 103 has received a call but he is not in the room. The caller would like to leave a message. The message is "call Josh at 215-555-1115." What do you do?

2) Housekeeping calls the front desk to place a maintenance order. It seems the wallpaper is peeling from the wall and the left leg on the desk is cracked in room 204. Record the maintenance requests in the PMS.

   Answer: The student should enter two separate work orders for these two problems.

3) Fred Phixit calls to say that the chair in room 204 has been replaced. What do you do?

   Answer: The student should record the work order for the chair as completed.

Answers to Chapter 5 Exercises

1) Room condition: dirty, clean, and inspected
Room status: vacant and occupied

2) The normal process for changing the room status occurs automatically during the night audit. The systems handles the change of the status from inspected to dirty to all occupied rooms as a normal part of the night audit.

3) 10- 11 this number may vary based upon homework assignments;
14- 15 this number may vary based upon homework assignments;
100, 102, 103, 104, 105, 107, 108, 110, 200, 201, 206, 207, 208, 301, 302 although this list may vary based on the students homework assignments;
100, 103, 104, 108, 110, 201, 202, 204, 208, 303

5) 10- 11, this number may vary based upon homework assignments;
14- 15, this number may vary based upon homework assignments;
100, 102, 103, 104, 105, 107, 108, 110, 200, 201, 206, 207, 208, 301, 302 although this list may vary based on the students homework assignments;
None

6) There are none listed

7) Enter H for Housekeeping and M for Maintenance. Now create a work order and describe it, as remote control does not work.

8) There is no work order entered for this item. Therefore, the student must enter the work order and record it as completed.

9) 110; TV remote does not work is the only outstanding work order

10) Enter a new message for Ms. Chrissy in room 208 and the message includes the words "please call the shop ASAP." Press T for telephone and 4 for new messages.

11) Enter a new message for room 108 and record the words "please call your mother when you get in." Press T for telephone and 4 for new messages.

12) Press T for Telephone and 7 to scan all messages.
Javed Muhammadi Room 104 "Call the Office"
Jeff Sullivan Room 100 "Call Office at 999-0909"
Haywood Eubuzzoffsky Room 108 "Please call your mother when you get in"

13) 104; The student should not give out the guest's room number. Rather s/he should instruct the person asking for the guest to pick up a house phone and call the front desk. Then the front desk can connect the caller to Mr. Muhamadi's room.

Transparency Masters for the Chapter 5 Workbook figures can be found beginning the next page.

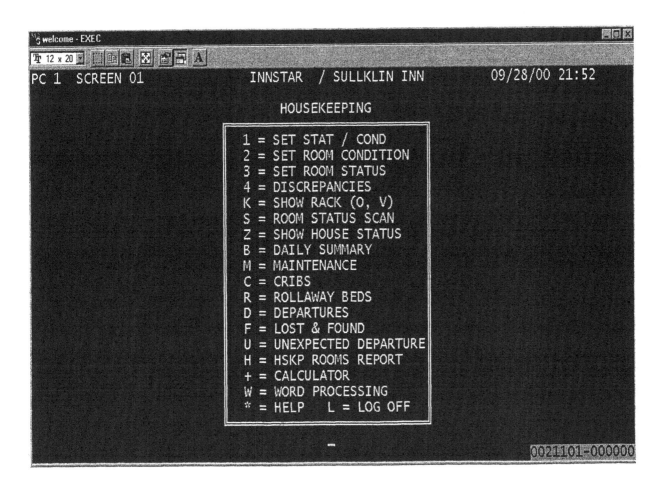

Figure 5.1

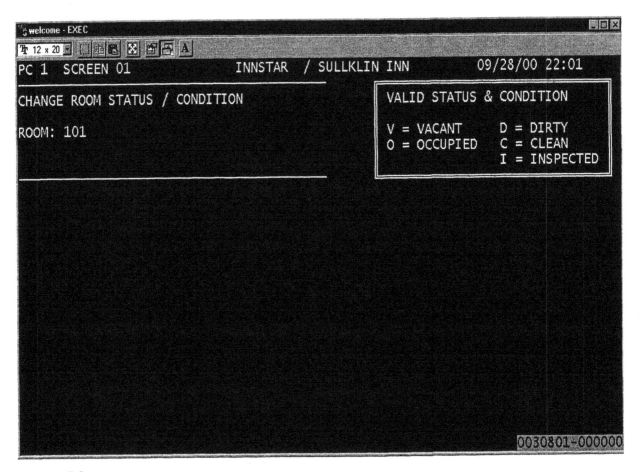

Figure 5.2

88

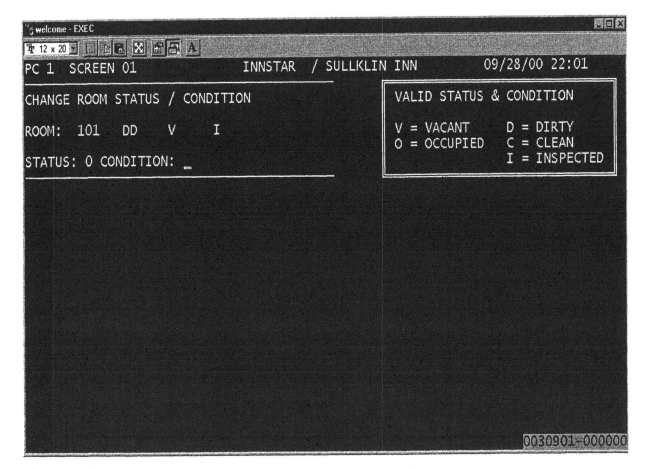

Figure 5.3

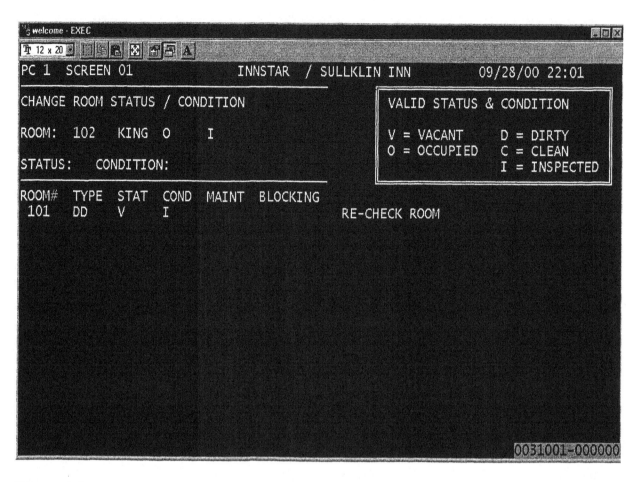

Figure 5.4

90

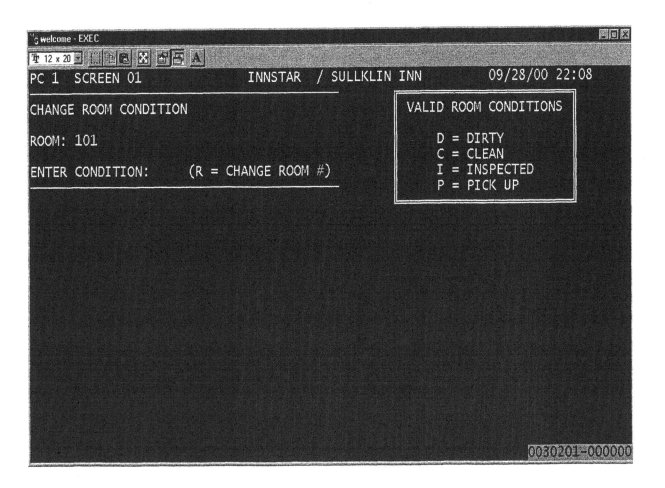

Figure 5.5

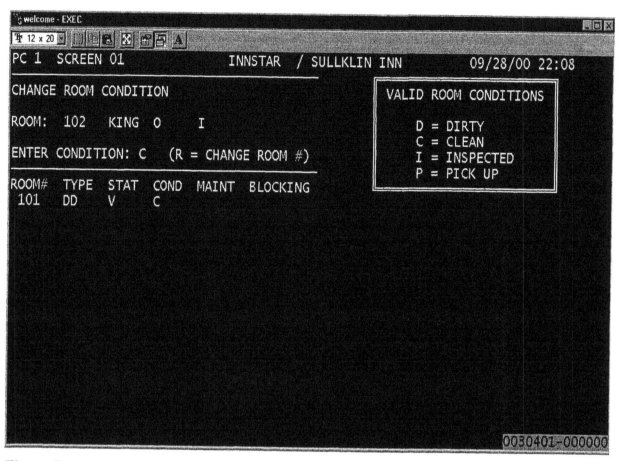

Figure 5.6

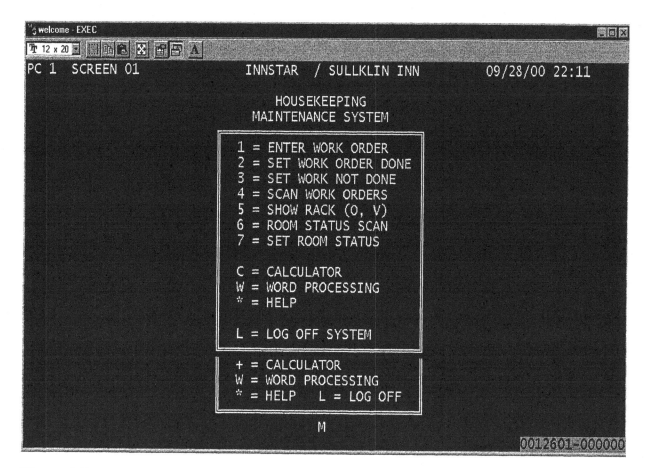

Figure 5.7

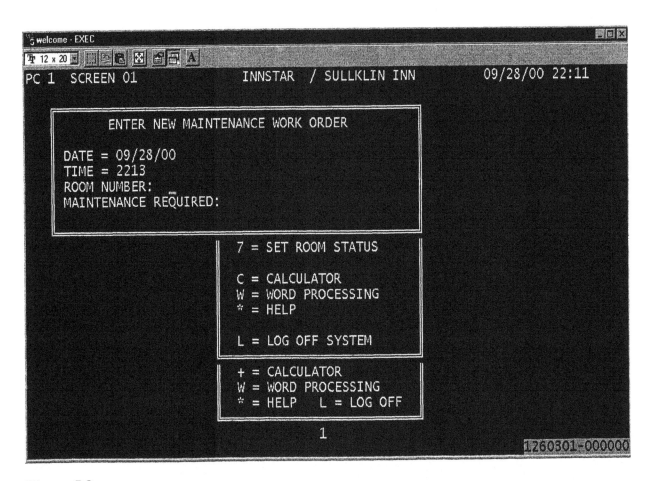

Figure 5.8

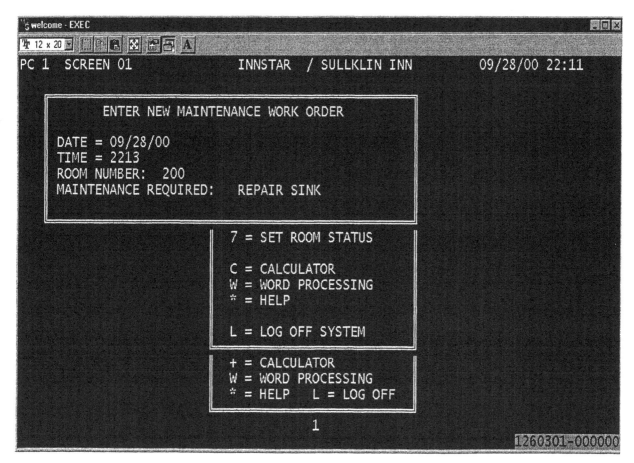

Figure 5.9

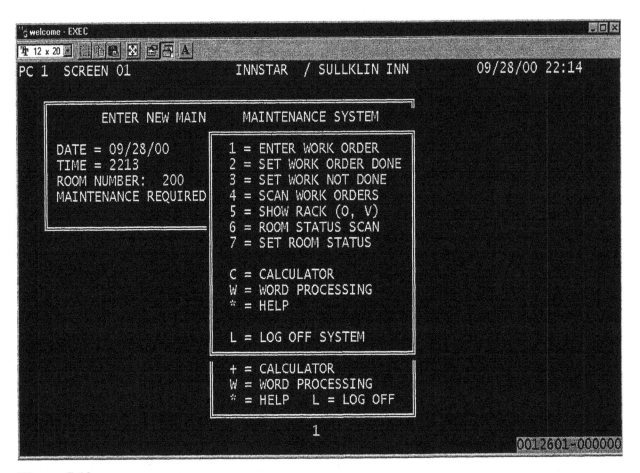

Figure 5.10

96

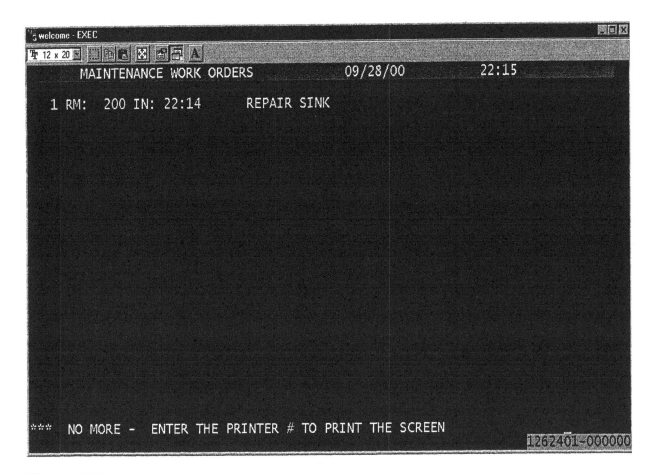

Figure 5.11

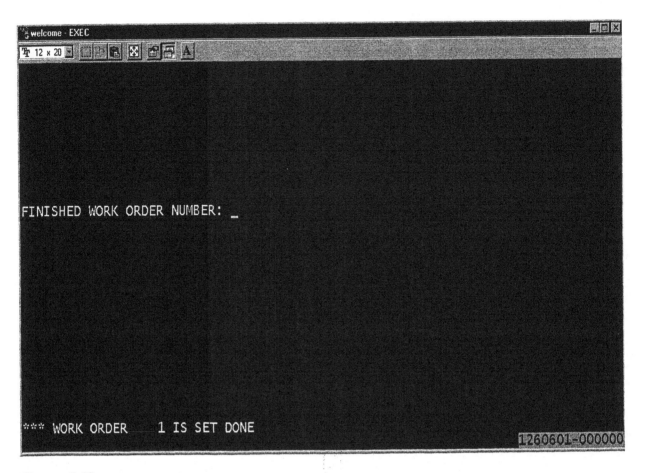

Figure 5.12

98

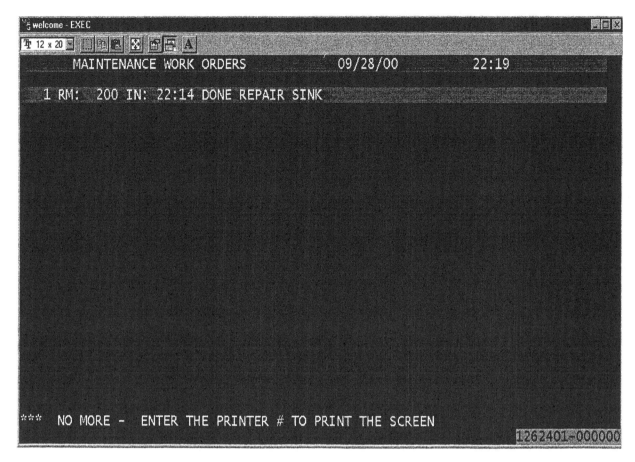

Figure 5.13

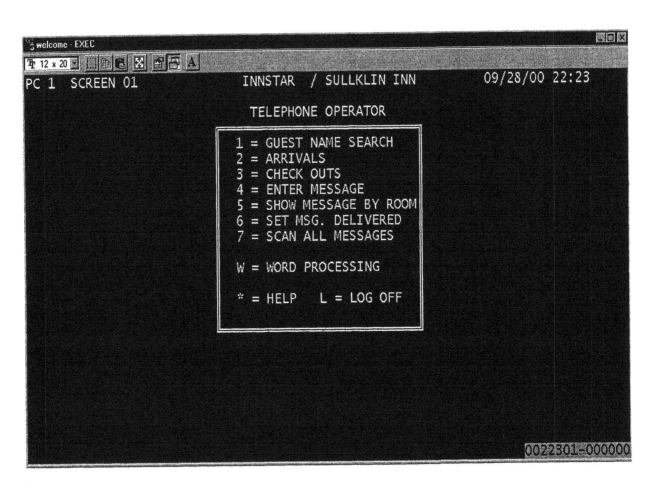

Figure 5.14

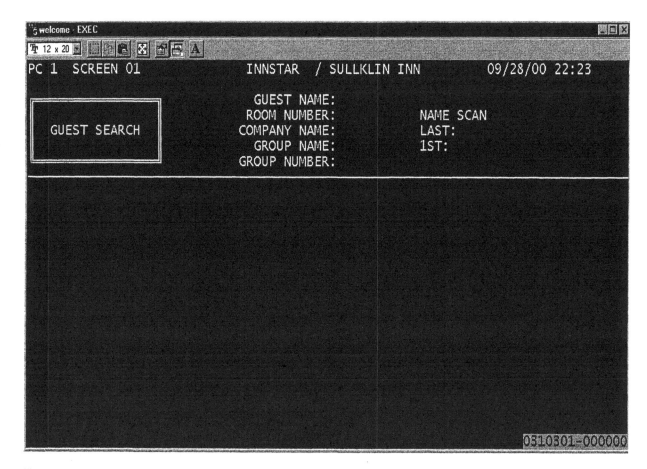

Figure 5.15

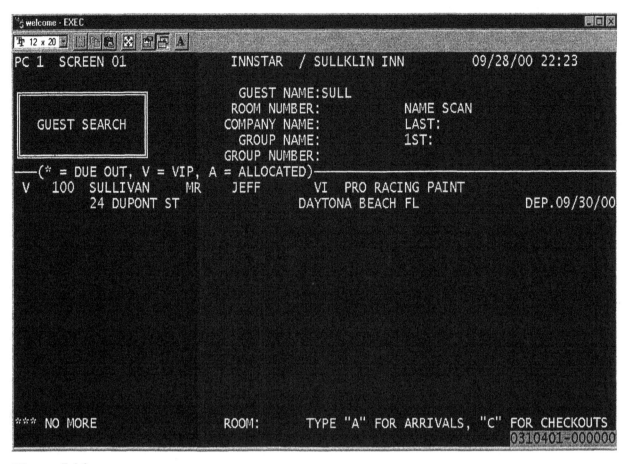

Figure 5.16

102

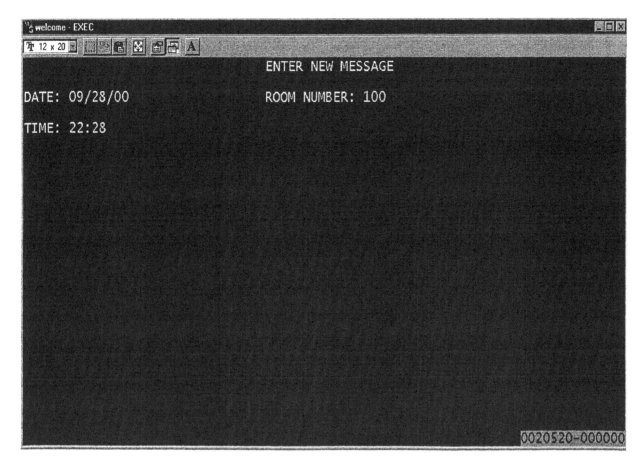

Figure 5.17

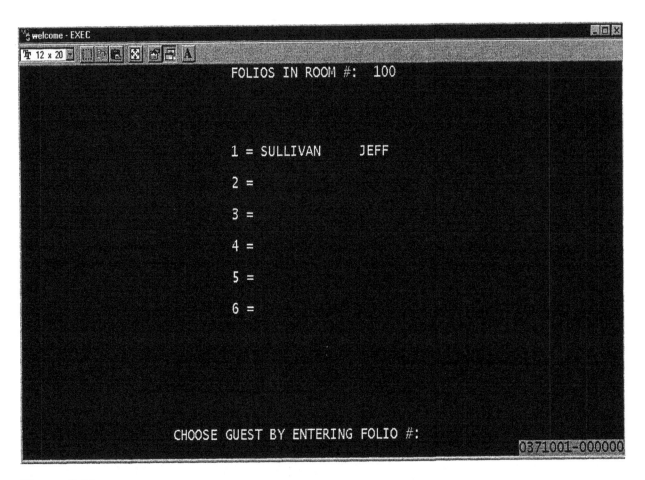

Figure 5.18

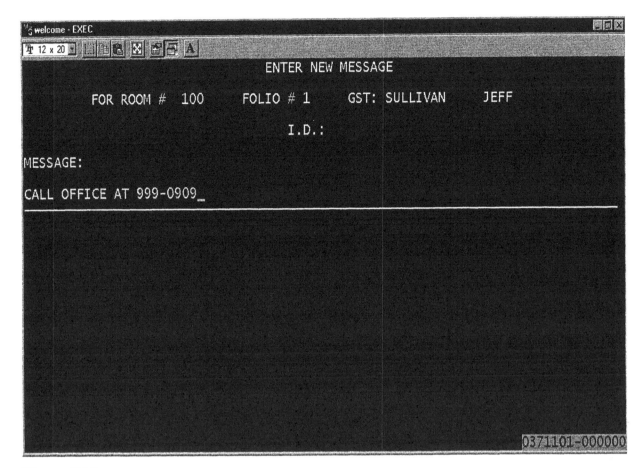

Figure 5.19

105

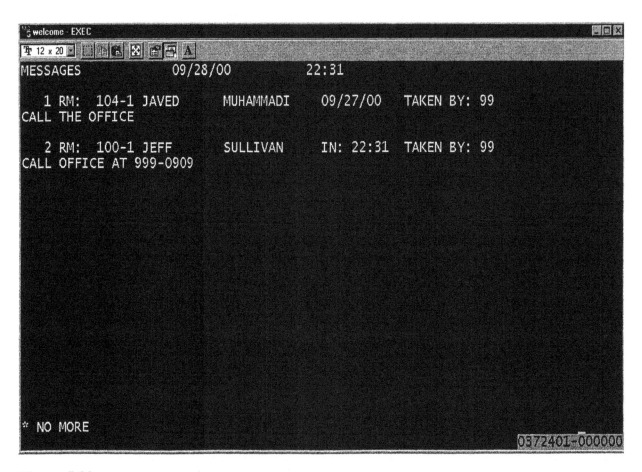

Figure 5.20

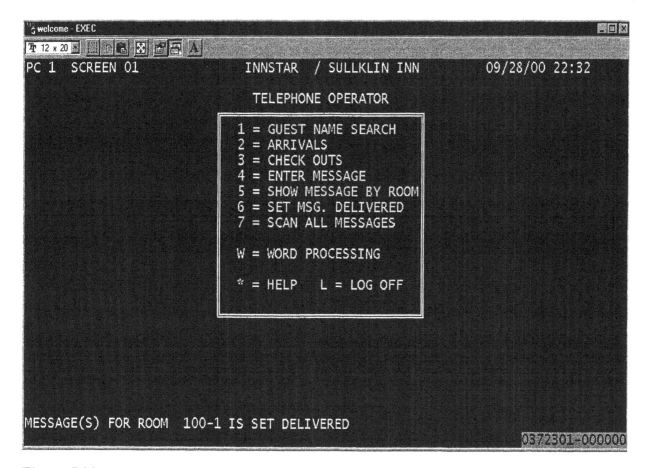

Figure 5.21

CHAPTER 6

NIGHT AUDIT

Chapter Outline

The last chapter is Chapter 6 the Night Audit chapter. A full night audit is run and reports are discussed in detail. Students learn how to read the reports. They gain a basic understanding of the steps involved in doing the night audit. Room charges and room taxes are posted during this process. At the end of the night audit the system date changes.

Key Learning Concepts in Chapter 6

- Review the purpose of the night audit.
- How to run the night audit using INNSTAR
- How to post room and tax
- Review key printed reports
- Analyze end of the day reports

Additional Activities and Exercise Suggestions

1) Summarize the purpose and use for each night audit report.

2) Have students answer the same questions for their prints outs of the night audit.

3) What is the room revenue amount for today?

   Answer: $1335.00

Answers to Chapter 6 Exercises

The answers to these questions are based upon the print out in the back of the book. Students may have a variety of answers to these questions based upon their respective night audit print outs.

1) The Night Audit is done review guest and non-guest accounts, and ensure that all transactions are recorded and are correct. After the night audit is completed the date in the PMS changes to the next day.

2) Posting room and tax and verify account balances.

3) Room 100 Sullivan -$15.00
   Room 103 Levy $10.00
   Room 106 Tanaka $15.00
   Room 201 Graw –$15.00

4) a) Levy
   b) Room 201 correction on a fax and Room 202 correction on a movie

5) a) $1527.20
   b) ($603.75)

6) Check-outs:
   Dottie Colm
   Arnold Thornberry
   Lauren Williams

   No shows:
   Nan Manifest
   Peter Murky

7) Room 200, repair sink
   Room 210 remote control is not working

8) 13.052%

9) $102.69

10) The occupancy percentage is very low and therefore this day would not be considered a good
    day. The ADR is good because the hotel didn't have too many comps. Or discounted rates.

To review the Night Audit Reports, refer to the Reports in Chapter 6 of the Workbook.

Made in the USA
Coppell, TX
30 November 2020

42509500R00063